What people are saying about *Firing Lousy Board Members*...

Famously half of Unilever's advertising ⟨ ... *half. Half our boards don't work, and h⟨* ... *fired, yet we know which ones all too we* ... *sector a massive service with this book.* ⟨...

Ken Burnett
Author, *Relationship Fundraising, The Tiny Essentials of an Effective Volunteer Board*, et al.

At last! The long-overdue guide to making dreams of nonprofit organizations come true by exorcising the nightmare of lousy board members. Simone Joyaux's lifetime of thoughtful, proven experience in building strong organizations is distilled in this highly readable, how-to road map to success. Read it, then get started today on building great boards and culling bad board members.

Roger M. Craver
Editor, *The Agitator*

Ask yourself which is the priority, the mission or the problem board member? Mission must be the answer! Simone Joyaux's concise, direct, clear guide gives you the road map to build a power board and confront problem members who jeopardize your mission.

Robbe Healey, MBA, ACFRE
Vice President for Philanthropy
Simpson Senior Services

Firing a nonprofit board member? Awkward! But it may be a little easier after you read this book by the plain-talking but insightful Simone Joyaux who says that poor-performing trustees present a problem of board contamination.

Ruth McCambridge
Editor in Chief
Nonprofit Quarterly

As frank as the title, Simone Joyaux has again demonstrated why she is a leading (and needed) voice in our sector. Good and effective board behavior must be articulated and enabled. Bad board behavior must not be tolerated. As staff and volunteer leaders, this is our shared mission-critical responsibility. Preach, sister!

Sharilyn Hale, MA, CFRE
Principal, Watermark Philanthropic Advising
BoardSource Certified Governance Trainer
Immediate Past Chair, CFRE International

What a fabulous book! Great examples and discussion clearly articulate the roles and responsibilities for excellent leadership and offer solutions to those problems that we all experience and that distract us from focusing on our mission. I want it now for the CEOs and board members of every organisation I have ever worked with—and those I will work with in the future!

Kitty Hilton, CFRE, FFINZ
New Zealand

In her new book, Simone Joyaux tackles the subject nobody wants or dares to discuss, namely firing lousy board members. Not only does she tackle it, but she explores it fully and succinctly with words of wisdom for all of us in the sector. I know it's trite to issue the phrase "required reading" in reference to any new book, but this one should be read and a quiz *given for every existing and future board members of all charities!*

Jay B. Love
Senior Vice President of Avectra
CEO/Cofounder of Bloomerang

On so many boards, we live through the parable of the boiled frog. Simone Joyaux shocks us with her ability to call our dysfunctions by name. With sincerity and honesty, she speaks truth to our power and asks us to use our common sense and our intelligence—our power—to be intentional in making the boards we want to serve on.

Anne Peyton, CFP, CFRE
Yellow Brick Road Consulting
Strafford, Vermont

Simone Joyaux is a unique combination of personal trainer, prophet, and agent provocateur. Her latest book tackles one of the great taboo subjects— dealing with weak volunteer leaders by sending them packing—with a kind of forthright wisdom that will take your breath away. Buy it, read it, use it.

Andy Robinson
Author, *Great Boards for Small Groups*

Set aside the provocative title, this manual is a succinct, no-nonsense guide to effective governance. Some books stay on the shelf. This will be on your desk and will be well thumbed. An invaluable resource and an external voice urging the courage to take action. Share this manual liberally. Your organization's mission will be best served.

Pearl Veenema, FAHP
President and CEO
Hamilton Health Sciences Foundation

Firing Lousy Board Members

And Helping the Others Succeed

Simone Joyaux

Firing Lousy Board Members

One of the **In the Trenches**™ series

Published by
CharityChannel Press, an imprint of CharityChannel LLC
30021 Tomas, Suite 300
Rancho Santa Margarita, CA 92688-2128 USA

CharityChannel.com

ISBN Print Book: 978-1-938077-42-5 | ISBN eBook: 978-1-938077-43-2

Library of Congress Control Number: 2013947207

13 12 11 10 9 8 7 6 5 4 3 2 1

Printed in the United States of America

This and most CharityChannel Press books are available at special quantity discounts for bulk purchases for sales promotions, premiums, fundraising, or educational use. For information, contact CharityChannel Press, 30021 Tomas, Suite 300, Rancho Santa Margarita, CA 92688-2128 USA. +1 949-589-5938

Publisher's Acknowledgments

This book was produced by a team dedicated to excellence; please send your feedback to editors@charitychannel.com.

We first wish to acknowledge the tens of thousands of peers who call CharityChannel.com their online professional home. Your enthusiastic support for the **In the Trenches**™ series is the wind in our sails.

Members of the team who produced this book include:

Editors

Acquisitions Editor: Linda Lysakowski

Copy Editor: Jill McLain

Production

In the Trenches Series Design: Deborah Perdue

Layout Editor: Jill McLain

Administrative

CharityChannel LLC: Stephen Nill, CEO

Marketing and Public Relations: John Millen and Linda Lysakowski

About the Author

Simone P. Joyaux, ACFRE, is described as one of the most thoughtful, inspirational, and provocative leaders in the philanthropic sector worldwide. She has guided countless organizations and professionals through her consulting and coaching, teaching, and writing.

Simone provides consulting services in fund development, strategic planning, and board development to all types and sizes of nonprofits. She speaks at conferences worldwide, and she serves as faculty for the Masters Program in Philanthropy and Development, Saint Mary's University of Minnesota.

As a volunteer, Simone founded the Women's Fund of Rhode Island, a social justice organization. She regularly serves on boards, including CFRE International and Planned Parenthood of Southern New England.

Her books, *Keep Your Donors: The Guide to Better Communications and Stronger Relationships* (coauthored with Tom Ahern) and *Strategic Fund Development: Building Profitable Relationships That Last*—now in its third edition—receive rave reviews and are considered standards in the field.

Simone has contributed chapters to other books: *The Fundraising Feasibility Study, (Me)Volution,* and *The Nonprofit Consulting Playbook: Winning Strategies from 25 Leaders in the Field,* from CharityChannel Press. Simone is also a popular web columnist for *The Nonprofit Quarterly,* publishes a free e-news, and blogs as Simone Uncensored.

Simone and her life partner give to philanthropic organizations annually and have bequeathed their entire estate to charity.

Dedication

I dedicate this book—and all of my writings—to those who are ambitious. And when I say "ambitious," I mean the individuals and organizations that care enough to challenge the status quo, ask the most cage-rattlingest of questions, foster conversation to produce learning, and then fight to make change.

I dedicate this book to those individuals and organizations that realize mission alone doesn't make a sustainable and effective organization. This book is for those who struggle—and demand—excellence in everything else, not just in mission.

Author's Acknowledgments

With respect and admiration, I acknowledge all the organizations and individuals I've worked with since 1975, when I first began my life's work in the nonprofit sector.

You've helped me develop my own personal mission and vision. You've helped me develop my skills and expertise. You've challenged me—as I hope I've challenged you. You've inspired me—and I hope that I have done the same for you.

Thank you to my staff colleagues at the former Arts Council Center in Lansing, Michigan and to those at Trinity Repertory Company in Rhode Island. Thanks to my clients, their staff, and boards.

Thanks to the volunteers and professionals in my workshops, and my colleagues and students at Saint Mary's University of Minnesota. Thanks to my fellow board members on all those boards over all these years, and my committee partners in various venues.

And thanks to Tom Ahern, my life partner and sometimes business associate. You taught me to write.

Contents

Summary of Chapters

Chapter One: Yes, Fire Them! The health of the organization matters the most, so firing bad performers is both acceptable and necessary.

Chapter Two: Who Is "You"? Is It "Me" or Someone Else? Who does the firing? This isn't a staff function, although the CEO has a role. And the board and governance committee have roles too.

Chapter Three: Serving on a Board Is Serious Business. Board service is a serious business and must be treated as such. Sadly, too many organizations—and their board members—think all is well, or not bad enough to fix.

Chapter Four: What, Exactly, Is Lousy? Lousy performance is not necessarily intentional. But sometimes it is!

Chapter Five: The Board Is Different from the Individual Board Member. The board member is different from the board. The concepts are not interchangeable, and the distinctions matter.

Chapter Six: Finding the Right Board Members. Finding the right board members reduces the need for firing. Make sure your process is intentional, focused, and clear.

Chapter Seven: Helping Board and Board Members Succeed. Helping board members—and the board itself—succeed is vitally important. Staff members play a central role in this success.

Chapter Eight: Monitoring Performance. Monitoring performance—and providing feedback—is an essential component of success.

Chapter Nine: The Chicken Way Out. Are you serious about strengthening the board? Or are you chicken?

Chapter Ten: Finally, Feedback Time. You don't really fire a board member. First you try to enhance attrition. If that doesn't work, you thank and release.

Conclusion: This Sure Takes a Long Time! Yes, this takes a long time, lots of attention, and gracious care. You can do it. You must do it. The health and effectiveness of your nonprofit depends on doing all this well.

Foreword

I'm going to buy a carton of these books, or manuals, as Simone calls them, so that I can give one to every executive director and board member of every organization I work with. What's in this book is *that* important.

The title, *Firing Lousy Board Members... And Helping the Others Succeed*, made me laugh because I've so often said that the biggest challenge of working with volunteers is that you can't fire them.

In this book, Simone proves me wrong! And if we take Simone's lessons to heart, the rewards will be huge.

Our organizations will function better... much better.

We'll do more good.

And we'll have more fun!

In this engaging book, full of stories and strong images, Simone explains that oft-neglected subject of governance. Do you find yourself nodding off whenever you read (or hear) that word, "governance"? If so, you're not alone.

Governance is a topic too often ignored. Who does it? What is it? And what difference does it make anyway?

But in this book, Simone has made "governance" fascinating and has helped me understand just how important it is.

This book is not really about firing volunteers. It's a book about how to govern an organization so you don't have to fire them. The irony is that well-governed organizations set up policies so that they can fire people! But an organization that has its act together well enough to do that is unlikely to have to do it.

Simone has written a book about power and accountability and clarity of intention. She helicopters up to thirty thousand feet to give us the all-important broad picture of how effective governance works, clarifying the roles of executive directors, individual board members, and boards as a whole.

Then she swoops down to the ground and provides just the tools you'll need to get your organization working at top governance capacity.

Not only are the appendixes full of material you can use, but the entire book has references throughout so that just when you are thinking, "I wonder how to do that?" there it is—a link to the answer.

I found this book to be both uplifting and sobering—a great combination. Uplifting because I finally understood that by using basic practices of sound governance, any nonprofit worth its salt can become great and accomplish more. Sobering because I realized that governance, like most things worthwhile, takes time and attention and effort. It's not easy or quick. But it is worthwhile!

Thank you, Simone, for writing this little book that finally makes the power and importance of good governance easily available to all.

Hey, you nonprofit leaders and board members... Read this book!

It will change the way you think and the way you function. And you and your organizations and the world will be better off for it!

Andrea Kihlstedt
Author, Speaker, Trainer, and Sage

Introduction

How many times have you sat in a boardroom and wished you were someplace else?

How many times did your wish relate to others in the room? Maybe some particular person?

Well, we've all been there. I suspect that every single individual who ever served on a board, or worked with one, has—at one time or another—wanted to eject some other board member from the boardroom.

Sometimes that's no big deal. The feeling is only momentary. I was annoying and you were annoyed. But we both got over it. You were silly and I was tired. But we both shaped up well at the next board meeting.

But sometimes... sometimes the wish to eject someone happens over and over. Sometimes you want that one person gone, permanently. That board member really is a real problem... really.

A Small Inconsequential Distraction... or Something More?

There's a difference between periodic disconnects, little annoyances, momentary frustration—and seriously bad regular behavior. There's a difference between different personalities and different styles—and regular dysfunctional performance.

I'll bet you know the difference. Most people mostly do. Most people understand when someone needs to be fired from the workplace. Or when that someone is actually doing a fine job and everyone just needs to be more accepting.

But too often, we do nothing about that bad behavior and too-regular dysfunctional performance. Why? Because we're scared to hurt someone's feelings or lose their gift or make them mad. Because we're afraid of conflict and confrontation. Because this is our volunteer work, and volunteer work is supposed to be fun, and firing someone isn't fun, so let's not do it. Because, after all, we're just volunteers, and this is just a nonprofit organization where we volunteer, so let's avoid the tough stuff.

Too often, we do nothing about the bad behavior and the often-frequent dysfunctional performance. Why? Just because.

Compromising the Organization's Quality

So we compromise the organization. We don't say that, of course. We won't even acknowledge that that is what we're doing. We hide our heads in the sand. We frustrate all the good board members. We put up with inappropriate behavior and dread attending board meetings. That's a downward spiral.

For me, a compromised organization is unacceptable. For me, absolving you and me from our accountability obligation—that's a sin of omission. And sins of omission are just as bad as sins of commission. Especially when, together, you and I could have made the organization stronger. But, instead, we weakened the organization. This shared inaction can cause the organization to flounder and wither. This lack of accountability produces an organization that is not as good as it could be.

For me, all of those "becauses" simply are not acceptable. I understand it's hard. I sympathize. But we're talking about the health and effectiveness of an organization. We're talking about the ability to deliver on mission and contribute to community. Doing all that—ensuring the organization's health and effectiveness, delivering mission impact, and making a difference in the community—may require firing someone.

Now Is the Firing Time

This manual is about the firing time. The bad behavior and dysfunctional performance. The unacceptable situation that causes harm to the organization. The time when others start to leave because of that one person who stays.

Serving on a board is a business proposition. Yes, of course, board service is commitment to mission. But for the board and staff, commitment to mission focuses on carrying out mission and—and it's a big "and"—doing business well too.

What are all those business things? Management and governance. Fund development and marketing/communications. Finance. And so much more.

Board members must pay attention to all those business things. Of course, the board focuses on mission. But focusing on everything else is just as important. The board ensures the quality of management and governance, fund development and marketing/communications, finance and facilities, legal and regulatory compliance... and more. Anything less is unacceptable. And anything (or anyone) that inhibits the effectiveness and efficiency of doing all this business stuff is a problem.

So back to that boardroom. You're ready. You'll graciously cope with the sometimes-annoying board member. Because you can be annoying sometimes too. But you want the bad performer gone. You want the board cleared of bad behavior, rampaging rogues, and everyone else who regularly disrupts board meetings and compromises the integrity of this business work.

You want this fixed fast. That's why you bought this manual, right? The title says it all: "firing lousy board members... and helping the others succeed."

Easy-to-Follow Recipes

You're hoping for an easy-to-follow recipe. You want practical tips and useful strategies. You might even want a guarantee. You know... "No one will be mad." "The fired board member will still give money, lots of money." "No bad press."

Well, there's good news and bad news. No surprise, eh?

This manual describes an approach and outlines steps. This manual gives you key principles, practical tips, important insights, and to-do lists. And this manual warns you when to watch out! By the way, lots of these are quick-to-read sidebars.

In some ways, this manual gives you some recipes. But nothing is particularly easy to do. And I can't promise that everyone will be happy.

A Ban on Quick Fixes and Silver Bullets

I want all my writing to help organizations and individuals succeed—and feel better too. I want all my writing to give you practical tips and useful strategies. And I want all my writing to help you understand "why," not just "how."

The world is too full of "how" and not enough "why." As if merely knowing how to do something—without context or understanding—will produce anything more than mediocrity... if that!

People want quick fixes and silver bullets. Sometimes just because people are impatient. Sometimes because others (e.g., your boss, my client, the board) demand immediate results. Sorry. Rarely do quick fixes and silver bullets exist, let alone work well.

How do any of us think we can do good and meaningful and lasting work with this unrealistic and subversive approach?

We can't. And I fight that every day as a consultant, teacher and trainer, and writer. Sure, I'll give you tips and strategies. Sure, I'll share with you lots of hows. But you'll have to listen to my whys too.

I can't make this easy for you. Not as a writer or consultant. But hopefully, I can make it less worse for you.

I've done everything I'm suggesting in this manual. I've done it as a staff person facilitating the process with my board's governance committee. I've done this as a board chair and governance committee chair. Everything I've outlined here does work.

So here it is, a candid resource manual for the board, its governance committee, the chief executive, and board members who want to make change. I hope this manual helps you and your organization.

Chapter One

Yes, Fire Them!

IN THIS CHAPTER

- ···→ What makes someone a lousy board member?
- ···→ Firing volunteers is okay
- ···→ Don't let their money stop you
- ···→ Yes, this approach works

Yes, your organization should fire nonperforming board members.

Did I just say something mean? Was I nasty?

Let's analyze each word.

"Firing." Of course, people need to be released for poor performance. But only after you've tried pretty much everything else first. No one deserves to be fired without due cause. No one deserves to be fired without respectful conversation.

"Lousy." Sometimes people just don't understand the job. How well did you explain the job before the person was hired? How well do you support and guide the person? How good is your feedback to enhance performance? Or is the person really behaving badly?

Oh, and by the way, "lousy" doesn't necessarily mean obnoxious. Some lousy board members are wonderful people. But...

> **Product Warning!**
>
> Don't carry this book around in front of your board members. It might be too scary! Maybe the publisher will offer a special plain brown paper wrapper. Then you can choose on or off, depending upon the circumstance or situation!
>
>

Here's my bottom line: No one person takes precedence over the health of the organization. Poor performers—lousy ones—don't get to stay. Poor (or lousy) performers harm the organization, whether they are paid employees or volunteers.

Ah, "volunteers." Is that the problem? You're afraid to release poor-performing volunteers? Why? Because you aren't paying them so they have no obligation to do a good job? You aren't paying them so they get to do whatever they want, even if it makes a mess?

Maybe you're okay with firing "regular volunteers" but not board members. After all, board members are really special, right?

Hmm ... I don't think board members are more special than any other volunteer. All volunteers are donating their time, and that's pretty special. Donating time is just as important and valuable as donating money.

Smart, effective, quality organizations do not accept financial contributions that conflict with mission and plans. And smart, effective, quality organizations do not accept gifts of time that cause problems.

Maybe you're okay with firing those "regular volunteers." But you're afraid to fire board members because board members are at the top of the ladder. Board members may be extraordinarily important people out in the world. You want that woman on your letterhead even though she causes problems at board meetings and in the office.

The Money Issue

And, of course, there is the money issue. How can you fire that board member when she gives you such a large gift? Oops, and we cannot fire that man who volunteers—even though he isn't on the board—because he is a big donor too.

So are you saying you'll do whatever it takes—even cause strife within the board, lose a competent staff person, annoy the high-performing board members—because you want the money? Are you saying that money trumps everything? That donors get to do whatever they want and you'll put up with it to keep their money?

You realize if you act like money trumps everything, people will notice. People inside and outside of your organization will figure it out. This behavior isn't much of secret.

In essence, you're saying to your high-performing board members that Mrs. Wealthy Smith gets to stay on as a board member, despite her poor performance, because she's got lots of money. But you might work up the courage to release Mr. Not-So-Much, a nonperforming board member, because his gift just isn't big enough to matter.

> ### Let Me Repeat
>
> Ultimately, no one person takes precedence over the health of the organization. Poor performers—lousy ones—don't get to stay. Poor (or lousy) performers harm the organization, whether they are paid employees or volunteers.
>
>
> important

And if money trumps everything, that will be obvious to those outside your organization. Some amazing board member candidates won't choose to play with you. Donors who don't see themselves giving major gifts will figure that you don't appreciate their gifts. And those donors will stop giving.

My Own Personal Pinnacle

Once upon a time… Sometime in the late 1970s.

I was the executive director of an arts center and community arts council in Lansing, Michigan. I wasn't teaching French or English in middle school or high school. That was my original career goal, but I never found a job. So I wandered and searched.

I was dumb enough and smart enough to apply for this executive director job. They were dumb enough and smart enough to hire me.

And I fell in love. I fell in love with arts administration. I fell in love with the nonprofit sector. And there it was, my life's work. (I figured that out about a decade later.)

Anyway, back to that beginning. I learned on the job. I learned by reading and attending conferences. I remember triumphs large and small. Failures big and little.

And I remember that one specific evening after the board meeting. I walked into my office, sat down on the floor in the corner behind my desk. And I cried and cried and cried. I cried so hard, I was dry retching. My program managers walked into my office and found me there. They were not surprised.

Yes, this was a fairly typical board meeting. Yes, I often felt demoralized and frustrated and angry and confused after board meetings. But this was the worst. Sitting on the floor in the corner rocking back and forth and crying and retching.

This was all about governance.

A few years passed. By late 1981, I was chief development officer at Trinity Repertory Company in Rhode Island. Trinity Rep was one of the nation's top regional theatres. Board members were more powerful and experienced than my board members back in Lansing.

I wasn't crying or crouching or retching. (Hmm ... I wonder if my CEO was? Nope, he wasn't. In fact, I knew he wasn't because I was his right-hand person for fund development, governance, and planning.)

I figured that the Lansing problem was mostly not my problem. I was partially right.

As the years passed, I looked in the mirror a bit more. I looked in the mirror a lot.

Governance problems don't belong just to the board. The board and its board members are not wholly responsible for problematic, inadequate, or poor governance. Staff is responsible too. In fact, I think that good governance starts with staff that enables good governance to happen. So I was responsible, too, for the Lansing situation.

Yes, the chief executive officer is responsible for enabling good governance to happen. Also, the development staff that works closely with the board and board members is responsible for enabling good governance to happen.

Look in the mirror first. I didn't back then. I do now.

Is This Approach Realistic?

Do you think maybe I'm naïve and unrealistic? Do you think I'm talking about some fantasy world?

Do you think that in the real world "firing lousy board members" just doesn't work?

Not true! On the contrary. This is about as real as it gets.

I've seen small grassroots organizations and major institutions fire lousy board members. I've been a board chair who has fired a lousy board member. I've chaired the governance committee when we've fired poor performers.

I've watched federal and local governments demand better governance, more accountability, and transparency. I've listened to public charity divisions of state government talk about setting up new laws and regulations because nonprofits just don't get it. I've heard donors complain about the governance scandals and the credibility of nonprofits.

And I'm reading (and writing) blogs, articles, and books that insist and demand (and beg) nonprofits (and for-profits) to fix themselves. I urge you to read articles in *Harvard Business Review, Nonprofit Quarterly*, and *Stanford Social Innovation Review*. Read the research presented in *The Chronicle of Philanthropy*. Develop yourself as a professional. Position yourself as an expert.

It's time—way past time—to get tough on boards.

So the nice, supportive, gentle me says: I know this can be hard. Lots of stuff is hard. But you and your organization can do this. Take a deep breath. Start slowly and carefully. Build understanding and ownership. You'll feel better, be proud, and be more effective.

The shock-and-awe me says: Get it together! Now. Your governments and your donors are getting frustrated.

Now combine nice, supportive, and gentle with and shock and awe. Use both with your organization. Learn and make change.

P.S. You've got nine chapters to read before you can—or have the right to—fire anyone. Come along with me now. Let's get started.

To Recap

◆ Firing lousy board members is part of good governance.

◆ Sometimes firing volunteers is necessary.

◆ Define "lousy" before any firing happens.

◆ No one—not even your biggest donor—gets preferential treatment.

Chapter Two

Who Is "You"? Is It "Me" or Someone Else?

IN THIS CHAPTER

···→ Learning about five different "yous" and their roles

···→ Organizational culture is important

···→ Introduction to my concept of "enabling"

···→ The CEO's job is tough—but that's the job

I use "you" throughout this manual. Grabs your attention, doesn't it? "Hey, you!"

As you read the upcoming chapters, I continually use the word "you." And I suspect you'll keep wondering who "you" is. So let's dispose of that quandary right now.

When I say "you," I am referring to one of five "yous":

◆ You, the organization

◆ You, the chief executive officer

◆ You, the board

◆ You, the governance committee

◆ You, the individual board member

"You" Refers to Your Organization

Your organization must establish policies and procedures for good governance. As important—perhaps more important—your organization must embrace a culture of excellence, growth, health, and sustainability. (I mean, really, what's the alternative? Embracing a culture of mediocrity and slow death?)

Think of culture as the personality of your organization, the way you all interact and behave. Corporate culture refers to the personality of an organization and the way its members interact and behave. Culture is pervasive, affecting all areas of the organization. Everyone within the organization helps transmit culture.

Here's one of my favorite definitions of corporate culture: "The set of rarely articulated, largely unconscious, taken-for-granted beliefs, values, norms, and fundamental assumptions the organization makes about itself, the nature of people in general, and its environment... organizational culture consists of the set of unwritten rules that govern acceptable behavior within and even outside of the organization" (Ian Mitroff, Richard O. Mason, and Christine O. Pearson, *Framebreak: The Radical Redesign of American Business* [San Francisco: Jossey-Bass, 1994].)

Although culture is too rarely discussed, it pervades an organization and is transmitted from one individual to another. Moreover, research shows that an organization's culture dramatically affects its effectiveness.

So what are your unwritten rules that guide behavior? What's your organization's personality? What do you all believe?

Here's what I hope: I'm hoping—and you should hope too—that your organizational culture recognizes the continuum of good to less good to simply bad performance by staff and volunteers. I'm hoping that your organizational culture embraces respect and candor and that it avoids the excessive congeniality that can cause dysfunctional politeness. I hope your culture reinforces high performance and ongoing and honest feedback. And I'm hoping that your culture embraces firing lousy anyone... after you've done all that can be done to change lousy to good.

Always remember: firing lousy board members does not depend solely on policies, procedures, and systems. Sure, these are important. But policies, procedures, and systems are only as good as the organization's culture. If the culture isn't right, then you'll just disregard policies, procedures, and systems. More specifically, if the culture isn't right, people will complain about and fight against the policies, procedures, and systems.

"You" Refers to the Chief Executive

No matter the title, your CEO is the key staff person. No matter the size, your CEO leads the organization, ensures effective operations, and provides guidance and support for the organization's mission and impact.

> **Learn More!**
>
> For more about corporate culture and organizational development, see my book *Strategic Fund Development: Building Profitable Relationships That Last*, 3rd ed. You'll learn about two business theories: systems thinking theory and learning organization business theory. You'll also learn about conversation as a core business practice and other valuable concepts and strategies for your organization.

practical tip

Equally important, the CEO provides guidance and support for the board to carry out good governance effectively. The CEO also provides guidance and support for the individual board member to participate in good governance well—and serve as a leadership volunteer outside of the governance process.

I call this process of guidance and support "enabling." Effective enabling is a critical responsibility of the CEO. Effective enabling is also a responsibility of the development officer, who engages board members (and other volunteers) in fundraising. I explain enabling in **Chapter Seven**, "Helping the Board and Board Member Succeed."

In order to effectively enable the board and its individual board members, the CEO must be knowledgeable about governance. Actually, I want the CEO to be an expert in governance. (And I expect the same of fundraisers. Fundraisers work closely with board members and, hence, must be able to help board members distinguish between governance and management.)

In addition to the governance body of knowledge (documented in articles, books, blogs, and research), I expect the CEO to serve on a board. There's nothing quite like direct experience to make the principles live.

The tough thing for the CEO is to lead and guide without usurping the board's authority. The CEO doesn't decide the policies, procedures, and systems for good governance. The CEO doesn't decide the board's job and the board member's performance expectations.

But the CEO does encourage the board to talk about good governance. The CEO does provide the body of knowledge to support the conversations. The CEO makes clear—graciously—that serving on a board does not mean knowing the body of knowledge. (Oh dear. Oh my. There are so many not-so-good and dysfunctional boards. Even the most prestigious organizations with the most sophisticated board members. Often these boards and their individuals don't know and perform good governance. Just look at all the scandals in for-profits and nonprofits. These scandals are not just management failures. These scandals are governance failures too.)

The CEO participates in these conversations with the board. The CEO is a peer to all board members. And if that peer relationship is not part of your corporate culture, explore why.

Maybe your board members don't understand the concept of "partnership" between board and CEO. Maybe your board members think they have to be totally responsible and directive.

CEO Job Description

Too many CEO job descriptions ignore the CEO's responsibility to know the body of knowledge for governance—and to provide leadership and support for good governance. And development officer job descriptions miss this concept too. See **Appendix A** for the CEO's job description. Also visit the Free Download Library on my website, simonejoyaux.com, to see the job description for the chief development officer.

practical tip

Maybe your CEO is not sufficiently competent to be treated as a peer. Then maybe there's another firing in your future. Maybe your board members are so arrogant that they don't see the CEO as a peer. Hmm … Some board member changes coming soon?

So, your CEO doesn't meet with the individual board member to provide performance feedback. Your CEO doesn't fire the lousy board member. Your CEO doesn't choose board members either. But your CEO has a voice in all that. Your CEO helps the board do this work.

"You" Refers to the Board

Sometimes "you" refers to the board, the group of people who are accountable for the health and effectiveness of the organization (in partnership with the CEO).

For example, the board adopts its job description. Of course, the CEO participates in the conversation and provides body of knowledge. The CEO may even draft the job description after the conversation. Then the board adopts the job description and holds itself accountable to perform accordingly. And the CEO consistently and continually enables the board to carry out that job description.

The same process defines the performance expectations of the individual board member. The CEO consistently and continually enables the board members to carry out the performance expectations. And the CEO raises concerns about individual board member performance in a conversation with the governance committee.

"You" Refers to the Governance Committee

Please don't use the term "nominating committee." It's old-fashioned and misrepresents the scope of work. Use the term "governance committee" or "board development committee" or "committee on trusteeship" or something like that. I choose to use the term "governance committee."

Another thought: sometimes I'll see an organization establish a subcommittee within the governance committee. And that subcommittee is a nominating committee.

I don't understand. There's no need for a subcommittee to handle board member and officer nominations. One of the jobs of the governance committee—part of its scope of work—is the process of identifying, screening, and nominating candidates for board member and officer positions.

The governance committee is a committee of the board. Committees of the board exist to help the board (the larger group) carry out governance activities. For example, the finance committee helps the board carry out its governance obligation to ensure the fiscal health of the organization. The fund development committee helps the board carry out its governance obligation to ensure the health of the organization through charitable giving.

Scope of Work for the Governance Committee

A board member chairs this committee. The CEO serves as staff to this committee, attends all meetings, and participates actively in committee deliberations. The governance committee reports to and is directed by the board itself.

The governance committee helps the board fulfill its due-diligence function to create the best board possible. The committee facilitates healthy development and operation of the board, its committees, and the individual board members.

Policy Role

The committee reviews and suggests adjustments to current board policies—and may also recommend new policies. Policies include role of the board, performance expectations of the individual board member, committee operations and limitations, board/CEO relationships, board composition, and so forth.

Assessment Role

Develop and carry out board and board member assessment processes. See, for example, the governance self-assessment in the Free Download Library at simonejoyaux.com. Conduct a governance assessment annually or biannually.

Your organization also needs a performance appraisal tool for the individual board member. See two different examples in **Appendixes C** and **D**.

Board and Committee Orientation and Development

The governance committee helps staff design an annual orientation for newly elected board members. As the year progresses, additional development opportunities might be helpful. Perhaps the board would like a workshop—at a regular board meeting—to discuss fundraising. The committee might bring in a special presenter for a particular issue. The committee might also recommend that board members attend community workshops.

Annual Board Election Process

Of course, the governance committee leads the annual election process. Key steps include the following:

◆ Set the context. Review the board job description, performance expectations of board members, and traits of a useful trustee.

◆ Identify needs. Given where the organization is at this point in time, identify the necessary skills and experience needed for board members. Review this list with the board to build understanding and ownership. Compare incumbents with requirements and identify any gaps. Prioritize this list and review with board.

◆ Evaluate. Evaluate incumbent directors based on a performance appraisal tool. Identify individuals who are not meeting expectations. If their terms are expiring, determine if you wish to renominate them or thank them for their contributions and release them. If you wish to renominate an individual whose performance has been weak, talk to the person first. Identify any barriers and help remove them if possible. Recommunicate expectations and explain enforcement.

◆ Identify and interview. Identify individuals to fill the gaps in skills and identify ways to access the individuals. Schedule interviews with selected candidates. Include a governance committee member and the executive director in the interviews. Conduct the interviews in accordance with the draft "script."

◆ Assess. With the full committee, assess the results of the candidate interviews. Select those candidates for election to the board. Select the slate of officers.

◆ Invite and confirm. Contact candidates and confirm their willingness to serve, adhering to the specified performance expectations. Reiterate expectations. Specify term length. Send a confirmation letter specifying the election date, date of board orientation, and regular board meeting dates.

◆ Nominate and elect. Present slate of officers and board members for election. Elect.

In summary, the governance committee helps the board carry out its governance obligation to ensure the health and effectiveness of the board work. That's lots more than the annual election.

"You" Refers to the Individual Board Member

There's a difference between the individual board member and the board. But most people don't seem to make this distinction. Too many people use the words interchangeably.

That's one of my pet peeves... the confusion between the board (the group) and the individual board member (who is part of the group). I regularly go through policies and procedures from organizations and have to separate the board and board member statements. See **Chapter Five**, "The Board Is Different from the Individual Board Member," in this manual to better understand the distinction.

The Bottom Line

I bet you want to know—right now!—who actually does the firing? My answer: a member of the governance committee. Usually, one single individual, representing the governance committee itself, has the face-to-face meeting.

But the firing doesn't happen till lots of other steps happen first. Without the first nine chapters of this manual operating well, you cannot fire anyone.

To Recap

♦ Pretty much everyone is responsible for ensuring an effective board and high-performing board members—and that includes the organization, the CEO, the board, the governance committee, and the individual board member.

♦ The CEO's role in governance is very important—perhaps more important than some people think.

♦ Organizational culture is critically important and not always sufficiently understood.

♦ The governance committee's scope of work helps ensure the board's effectiveness.

Chapter Three

Serving on a Board Is Serious Business

IN THIS CHAPTER

···→ How serious corporate governance is

···→ Make sure there's governance expertise on your board

···→ Opinion and expertise are different

Yes, your organization should fire nonperforming board members.

But not yet!

Successfully firing lousy board members is a major strategy to retain high-performing board members. Good performers don't want to waste time with bad performers. Good performers often leave boards that have bad performers. Good performers sometimes end up acting like bad performers (or at least less good performers): "You accept bad performers, so why should I bother working so hard to perform well?"

Successfully firing lousy performers builds a strong organization. Successful firing also helps establish a corporate culture (and norm) for good governance and good individual board member performance.

And, if done well, firing lousy performers keeps them as friends. Yes. The point is to fire well so you maintain positive relationships.

Of course, successful firing of bad performers means you must define good and bad performance. You must articulate standards and communicate them. You conduct screening interviews before nominating board members. You monitor and evaluate performance. You need ways to fire that don't cause pain—to the bad performers or your organization. You need the guts to do this.

Back to the Very Beginning

First, serving on a board is serious business. The board is accountable for ensuring the health and effectiveness (mission, fiduciary, etc.) of the corporation. That's what corporate governance means.

Serving on a board is not about having fun and hanging out with cool people. Serving on a board isn't just about showing your commitment to the cause. Show your commitment by giving money or volunteering to do some other kind of work.

Serving on a board is hard work that requires business acumen, strategic thinking, and the willingness to challenge staff and fellow board members. Serving on a board requires advance reading and regular meeting attendance. Serving on a board requires that board members inconvenience themselves to learn new stuff, to attend meetings when they'd rather celebrate Valentine's Day or a birthday.

> **Are You Overwhelmed Yet?**
>
> Do you think, maybe, it's easier to just keep them? No! Stop that kind of thinking right now. Just stop it!
>
> **watch out!**

Serving on a board is like being hired for a job. But you aren't paid when serving on a nonprofit board.

Since board service is that important and serious, inadequate performance is a serious offense. Repeated inadequate performance demands termination, just like in any job.

What Comes First?

Your chief executive and board members must understand that board service is serious business. This is the first weakness I find. In my experience, the chief executive and board members often don't understand the seriousness of governance.

I use two different approaches to help organizations, staff, and board members understand the importance of governance:

◆ Gracious, gentle approach. "How about a little health checkup to ensure that your governance is top notch? Let's assess your governance."

◆ Shock-and-awe approach (often the necessary choice). "Scandals abound in both for-profit and nonprofit sectors. Many of these scandals are governance failures. Governments are increasingly frustrated. They're inventing new laws and regulations. It's just a matter of time before donors get fed up too. Some already are. So let's make sure your governance is top notch."

Too many executive directors don't know the basic principles of corporate governance. Too many executive directors don't know how to help the board and its members do governance. In fact, too many executive directors see the board as a distraction, a frustrating idiosyncrasy required by government.

These executives don't recognize their leadership role. They complain about board performance but don't accept their responsibility for effective enabling. Some executive directors disempower their boards, denying governance accountability.

The bottom line: without accepting the seriousness of governance, you're in trouble. The other bottom line: without effective enabling by staff, it's difficult for boards to do governance well.

If your CEO isn't yet sufficiently experienced in governance, insist on professional development. Who insists? The board of directors makes this directive to the chief executive.

Recruit an experienced governance expert for your board. This individual adds important expertise to help the board do good governance. This individual can also serve as a mentor to the CEO.

Something to keep in mind: board service does not mean an individual is a governance expert. I think most boards don't do governance well, including the really sophisticated boards with all those high-powered important people serving. So those board members aren't expert. And perhaps they aren't even sufficiently adequate.

Opinion or Expertise?

There is a difference. And, yes, the difference really matters. Here's what I mean:

You either like or dislike Picasso's work. That's your personal view or attitude. But art experts (drawing on their body of knowledge, expertise, and experience) judge Picasso as a seminal artist, a game changer.

You hire a lawyer and pay attention to what this expert says without wasting too much time offering your ill-informed or uninformed opinions about the law. You hire a doctor and don't second-guess the physician's surgical methods.

There's a substantive difference between personal opinions, which are not based on expertise, and informed opinions, which are based on expertise and body of knowledge and research. Unfortunately, the nonprofit sector seems full of opinions, and far too many are the bad kind: ill informed and uninformed.

For example, your boss doesn't like the direct-mail letter you wrote. Your letter is based on the body of knowledge and research from the direct marketing gurus of the nonprofit and for-profit sectors. But your boss isn't "comfortable" with the letter. In the boss's opinion, the letter doesn't represent the agency well.

Who is the fundraising expert at your agency? Not your boss. (And not your board chair or any of your board members either, by the way!) The expert had better be the fundraiser.

Here's another example. Your board chair, the bank CEO, runs a tight board meeting. The chair uses the executive committee to work through all issues before the board meets. Committees report at each meeting. Board dialogue is limited. Your organization doesn't embrace conversation as a core business practice.

Executive Committees

I'm on a worldwide mission to destroy all executive committees. To learn why, see my web columns and article in the *Nonprofit Quarterly*, nonprofitquarterly.org. Check out my blog, Simone Uncensored, and my Free Download Library at simonejoyaux.com.

food for thought

As the executive director, you've studied the body of knowledge about governance by attending workshops and reading books and research. You also serve on boards. You're trying to improve governance at your agency— and that certainly includes board meetings. But your board chair graciously chuckles and says, "I've served on more boards than you are old. We'll stick with my tried-and-true approach."

Your board chair thinks that years of board service make an expert in governance and board development. But the chair is wrong. Experience alone doesn't make an expert. An expert needs the book knowledge and the research findings.

Too-Often Lousy Fundraising and Governance

There's something else that severely limits the quality of personal opinions and experience in fundraising and governance: the too-often lousy fundraising and governance that people observe and participate in . . . and then copy.

For example, I find that most boards are somewhat (or lots) dysfunctional. I'm talking about the supposedly sophisticated boards with their supposedly knowledgeable staff and their power broker board members. Yes. Most boards are not that good. And it's not just me who says so. Read the research and the for-profit and nonprofit sector publications like *Harvard Business Review* and *Nonprofit Quarterly*.

Another example: Fundraising isn't doing all that great either. There's the donor-retention crisis that began before the 2008 recession. The lack of knowledge about donor satisfaction. Insufficient personal face-to-face solicitation. Lousy donor communications. Too many fundraisers don't know the body of knowledge or follow research. And those who do too often get stymied by bosses and boards with personal opinions.

Living in a Fact-Free Zone Governance

There's another problem we have in our work—and in our society at large: fact denial and fact deniers.

"We live in a world where scientific knowledge is subordinated to political and religious dogma, where intellect and expertise are denigrated as elitist, where demands proliferate that history be taught as an exercise in national self-congratulation, not critical self-examination." So said Eric Foner in his May 13, 2012, commencement address for doctoral candidates at Columbia University, published in *The Nation* magazine, June 25, 2012, thenation.com.

> ### Science!
>
> There's actually a science of why we don't believe science. You absolutely must read Chris Mooney's marvelous article in *Mother Jones*, "The Science of Why We Don't Believe Science," motherjones.com/politics/2011/03/denial-science-chris-mooney.
>
> **principle**

Instead of respecting the body of knowledge and research, too many people assert their own opinions. And these people demand that all others accept the validity of their personal opinions. In fact, parts of our society (and our enterprises, no matter the sector) too often deny facts and assert opinion. Global warming, anyone?

Have you heard of the 2011 movie *Anonymous*? It's about Shakespeare not writing Shakespeare… the suspicion that someone else wrote Shakespeare… (And, most likely, only an English lord could write Shakespeare because how could a commoner like Shakespeare write something as great as Shakespeare!) In this movie, the author of Shakespeare is supposed to be Edward de Vere, 17th Earl of Oxford.

When the movie premiered, a *New York Times* op-ed (James Shapiro, October 17, 2011) wrote this about fact or fiction: "*Anonymous* offers an ingenious way to circumvent… objections: there must have been a conspiracy to suppress the truth of de Vere's authorship; the very absence of surviving evidence provides the case.

"In dramatizing this conspiracy, Mr. Emmerich [film director] has made a film for our time, in which claims based on conviction are as valid as those based on hard evidence. Indeed, Mr. Emmerich has treated fact-based arguments and the authorities who make them with suspicion. As he told an MTV interviewer… when asked about the authorship question: 'I think it's not good to tell kids lies in school.'"

Are you wondering which is the lie? Shakespeare or Lord de Vere?

Stop the Uninformed and Ill-Informed Opinions and the Fact Deniers!

So let me summarize, after this rather long rant! Uninformed or ill-informed personal opinion is irrelevant to the work we do. These opinions—too often promoted by whichever "powers that be" control your life or our agency or our world—stop forward progress. These opinions distract us from the right work, and they compromise integrity.

The job of good and competent professionals—and ethical leaders—is to graciously and forcefully disengage from uninformed and ill-informed opinions.

"Is everyone entitled to an opinion?" asks Seth Godin in his April 9, 2012, blog, sethgodin.com. Seth responds: "Perhaps, but that doesn't mean we need to pay the slightest bit of attention. There are two things that disqualify someone from being listened to... Lack of standing... No credibility."

Opinion or Expertise?

Check out Scott Adams' *Dilbert* cartoon from October 7, 2012...
"I like to have opinions. But not informed ones." (dilbert.com/strips/comic/2012-10-07)

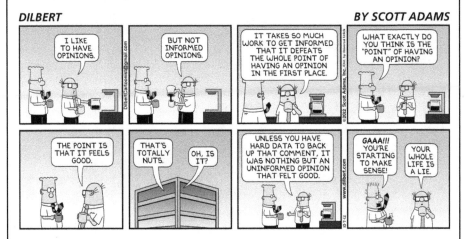

DILBERT © 2012 Scott Adams. Used By permission of UNIVERSAL UCLICK. All rights reserved.

PS: Maybe you need to show this entire section, "Opinion or Expertise," to your board members, your boss, your staff. Maybe you need to post the *Dilbert* cartoon in your offices and hallways.

You and I need to pay particular attention to "no credibility." As Seth notes, "An opinion needs to be based on experience and expertise." So you and I had better acquire and maintain that expertise and experience. And find board members who display that same respect.

To Recap

◆ Serving on a board is serious business. Behave accordingly.

◆ Opinion and expertise are different. Make sure you're using the right one at the right time.

◆ Make sure your CEO is very knowledgeable about governance.

◆ Serving on a board does *not* make someone a governance expert.

Chapter Four

What, Exactly, Is Lousy Performance?

IN THIS CHAPTER

- ---→ Are board members lousy on purpose?

- ---→ Three different kinds of lousy performance: unintentional, unaware, and intentional

- ---→ Anger and blame

Are these people being lousy on purpose? Do they even know they're performing lousily? (I like that word, "lousily." Even if it isn't a real word, it's my word.)

Let's calm down. I'll try to control my anger if you'll try to control yours! Because it's for sure that lousy performance makes me angry. I suspect it makes you angry too.

For sure, I can move into the blame game really quickly. So I have to take a deep breath. I have to look in the mirror and tell myself to "shape up" and "stop it."

I'm stepping back right now. Please, you step back too.

What, exactly, is lousy performance? And where does it come from?

I'm thinking of three different kinds of lousy: Unintentional lousy performance. Unaware lousy performance. Intentional lousy performance.

What do you think? How do you differentiate? How about having this conversation with the governance committee and the full board? Create a shared understanding. Establish a norm within your organization.

Unintentional Lousy Performance

Sam doesn't know what he doesn't know. He doesn't know what good performance looks like. He certainly doesn't know the body of knowledge, the general guidelines, etc. It might not even occur to Sam that there is a body of knowledge for corporate governance.

> ### Your Job!
>
> If you're the CEO, it's your job to effectively enable Sam. If you're a board member, ask yourself, is your CEO an effective enabler?
>
> **principle**

Sam is committed to the cause and the organization's impact. He always works hard. He always wants to do well at any job. He'd probably be very happy to know that there is a body of knowledge. He's probably willing to learn too.

It's up to you—the organization, the chief executive, the governance committee—to provide the information, guidance, training, and knowledge for Sam. And it is up to you—the board—to ensure that all this is in place and well implemented.

There's another kind of unintentional lousy performance. Sarah wants to perform well. She paid attention to the clearly articulated performance expectations. She attended the orientation and participates in board meetings. She listens well and tries.

Resources, information, and guidance are all available to Sarah. But she still doesn't quite get it. Her performance as a board member just isn't working so well. Maybe she isn't ready to serve on this board. Maybe she is distracted by other things in her life.

Give Sam a chance. You failed him. He hasn't failed you.

Give Sarah another chance. Help her. With stronger guidance, maybe she can improve her performance and become a good board member. Or maybe she can't. Good intentions and great effort do not always produce good results.

Unaware Lousy Performance

Pete mostly understands what it takes to operate effectively as a board and to be a good board member within the group. He raises difficult (and important) issues even when it's uncomfortable.

Pete is enthusiastic and sometimes rather overwhelming to fellow board members. He's not always adequately prepared for meetings and can push the agenda off the rails. Pete doesn't realize that sometimes he dominates conversations and repeatedly raises the same issue. He's kind of tough to control.

Board members like Pete often respond well to respectful and kind feedback. And one-on-one mentoring might help Pete too. But if not...

Intentional Lousy Performance

Now meet Keith. I don't mean that Keith is intentionally lousy. He actually thinks he is a good board chair.

So here's an important question for you: Who decides what constitutes good leadership, a good board chair? Ultimately, the board decides. The governance committee can start the conversation at its meetings.

The conversations about "what is good" depend upon some level of expertise, some knowledge about good governance and good group dynamics, and teamwork, etc.

Now back to Keith. Keith doesn't much care for the perspectives of others. He expects it's his right and responsibility to decide all sorts of things.

Keith runs board meetings the way he wants. Actually, Keith does pretty much anything he wants. In fact, Keith is clear that, as board chair, he has lots of rights.

Get Rid of the Rogues

Keith isn't a rogue like Johnny Depp in those pirate movies. Keith is a rogue elephant, rampaging around and doing harm. Don't pick a Keith in the first place. And if, inadvertently, you end up with a Keith, get rid of him. You're the board. You control your destiny. Sure, it can be hard to do. This is work. This is serious business. And if you keep a Keith, it's your own fault.

watch out!

He doesn't like conversation and restricts it at board meetings. He does the same at any committee meeting he attends. He does a lot of work behind the scenes, lining up the votes he wants and ignoring other voices.

Keith doesn't question his own assumptions about what's right. Keith doesn't appreciate feedback and doesn't listen to it. When I explained to Keith that his approach is not good governance, he disagreed with me. "But I know I'm right," he said to me. He didn't care about the body of knowledge. He didn't care about what makes groups effective or ineffective.

Keith is a rogue. Keith violates the concept of the board—the group— when he lobbies behind the scenes. In his flawed concept of leadership, Keith violates the concept of equity among board members. Keith is that rogue elephant rampaging around the room. And board members are accountable for letting the rogue elephant rampage. It's time to fire this lousy board chair.

To Recap

◆ Get out your spyglass to determine the type of lousy that's happening with your board members.

◆ Get angry carefully. And manage the blame game well. Remember, the blame might be yours.

◆ Fix what you can. That's the first way to intervene.

Chapter Five

The Board Is Different from the Board Member

IN THIS CHAPTER

···→ Distinctions between the board (the group) and the individual board member

···→ Relationship between the board and the board member

···→ Role of the board, its job description

···→ Performance expectations for the individual board member

You—all of you and every one of us who works with nonprofits and serves on boards—must understand the distinction between the board and the individual board member! I think this is one of the biggest problems in the sector. And it's no small problem. It's a huge problem. The hugest of the huge. (Yes, I've invented another word, "hugest.") The most fundamental of the fundamentals.

Almost every board I encounter is confused about this. Yes, just about every single board. That includes the most highly sophisticated boards with the most-experienced board members.

How do I know? I read their bylaws. I review their policies. I ask them questions. I listen to how they talk.

And guess what else? Just about everyone who writes about governance seems to use the term "board" and "board member" interchangeably.

I read comments like: "The board helps raise money." Not true! Board members help raise money. It's an individual activity. Yes, the board has a fundraising role. The board sets the goal, approves the strategy, and defines the board member role in fundraising.

Please fix this. Please acknowledge the distinction between the board and the board member. Talk about the distinctions enough until everyone gets it. Then speak and write correctly. And correct each other and yourself when you misuse the words "board" and "board member."

Please promise me. Honestly, this will help.

Distinguishing Between the Board and the Board Member		
This grid provides examples of the distinction between board work, the work of board members at board meetings, and the work of board members outside of board meetings.		
	The Individual Board Member	
The Board—the Group at Board Meetings	Inside Board Meetings as Part of the Group That Is the Board	Outside Board Meetings as a Leadership Volunteer
Establish charitable-contributions goals. Define board member performance expectations regarding fund development.	Review material in advance. Ask strategic questions. Engage in board conversation. Behave in a way that supports group process. Vote.	Give a financial contribution. Help identify those who might be interested in the cause. Help nurture relationships with donors. Help carry out fundraising activities.

Start with the Board

The board is a group. Corporate governance is a collective act. Governance happens only when the board is together, e.g., at its meetings. And only the board decides governance items. For example, the board is accountable for very specific things:

◆ Defining values, mission, vision, and strategic direction

◆ Ensuring financial sustainability by adopting a budget and fund development plan, and monitoring performance

◆ Hiring, appraising, and firing the chief executive

◆ Ensuring legal and regulatory compliance

Your board talks about the concept of corporate governance and the distinctions between the board and the individual board member. After the preliminary conversation(s), draft the job description of the board (often done by the CEO). Distribute the policy for further conversation, and then the board acts. Once adopted, adhere to the policy. Enforce it. Monitor the board's adherence to its job.

The board's job description is the first policy that moves you along the path to firing lousy board members. The job description of the board (the group) is the first building block, the foundation. Without a full understanding of the board's role—and how it is different from that of the individual board member—you cannot move forward.

See the sidebar, "Role of the Board." By the way, the job description of the board is pretty much the same for a nonprofit and a for-profit. And the job description of the board is the same for any nonprofit, no matter the size or industry or anything else!

Remember, corporate governance happens only when the board is together at its meetings. The board carries out its job description at the board meeting. That's challenging.

How do you operationalize the board's job description at the board meeting? Take a look at the Due Diligence Plan in the Free Download Library on my website, simonejoyaux.com.

The Individual Board Member

The board member is part of the group that is the board. The board member has no individual authority; only the board itself has authority.

No single board member is more important than any other board member. For example, that means that the board chair has no more authority than any other board member. And I cannot think of a single decision that the

Role of the Board

The board of directors is legally and morally (ethically) accountable for the health and effectiveness of the organization. The board ensures that the organization achieves its mission in an ethical, transparent, accountable, and prudent manner.

The board's job is governance, the ongoing process of due diligence whereby the board operates as a collective to ensure corporate health and effectiveness. Specifically, the board is accountable for the functions described below.

The board works in partnership with its chief executive (CEO). The executive provides leadership and support, enabling the board to carry out its governance responsibility.

Board Functions/Scope of Authority

All of this is accomplished as a group—at board meetings—through review of information, strategic questioning, conversation, and decision making.

1. Articulate values and mission, and set standards, controls, and policies. Ensure that all the organization's programs, activities, and operations adhere to these. .

2. Ensure that the organization is relevant to the community through processes that monitor the external environment and define vision, direction, and strategy.

3. Define and monitor key areas of performance compared with short- and long-range strategy/plans, assess results, and ensure that steps are taken for continuous quality improvement in all areas.

4. Ensure financial sustainability and intergenerational equity, e.g., operations, reserves, and capitalization.

5. Ensure that adequate risk management is in place, e.g., safety and security, insurance, data backup, CEO succession, board officer and board member succession, etc.

6. Define criteria for board membership, ensure proper recruitment of candidates, elect members and officers, and ensure proper orientation and development of board members.

7. Define and enforce parameters of the board's work, including its committees and task forces, and the role and performance of the individual board member. Assess effectiveness.

8. Define the role of and hire the CEO. Appraise performance; set compensation; reward competence; and, if necessary, replace the individual.

9. Ensure compliance with relevant laws and regulations affecting the organization

10. Ensure effectiveness of management without intruding in management's role and authority.

11. Act as a think tank and sounding board regarding organizational health and effectiveness and the marketplace environment without compromising management's authority.

Notes:

◆ Ken Dayton's monograph *Governance Is Governance* inspired this job description. It was published by Independent Sector, a nonprofit, nonpartisan coalition of approximately 600 charities, foundations, and corporate philanthropy programs. Its mission is to advance the common good by leading, strengthening, and mobilizing the nonprofit and philanthropic community. To learn more about Independent Sector, please visit: independentsector.org. Read Ken's monograph!

◆ Take a look at number eleven. As a group, the best board can serve as a "think tank" and "sounding board" for the organization and its CEO. The challenge is to ensure that the board, including its individual members, recognizes that this is neither a directive nor an authoritative function.

principle

board chair gets to make. Because anything that is governance must be decided by the board itself. And anything that is management belongs to the staff.

I say again: the board is a group. That's not some minor inconvenience. That's not something that can be ignored because a single individual is so brilliant. If that brilliant individual cannot play well with others, that individual does not belong on your board. Engage that brilliant individual elsewhere—perhaps with a single task—not as part of a group. This individual does not belong on your board.

The board member has responsibilities to the group. For example, each board member must prepare for and regularly attend board meetings. Board members must ask strategic questions and participate in board conversations.

The board member also has responsibilities beyond participating in the group that does governance. I think of board members as leadership volunteers outside the board meetings. For example, that means that each board member gives a personal financial contribution to the organization every year. That isn't a governance act. But it is a lead volunteer act. Every single board member helps with relationship building and fund development in some way. That isn't a governance act. But it is a lead volunteer act.

See the sidebar "Performance Expectations for the Individual Board Member." For me, these are fundamental principles. Pay particular attention to the expected behaviors. That is often the problem in performance. People have useful skills and expertise and contacts. But their behaviors don't contribute to group effectiveness. And the board is a group.

I use the term "board member" for the individual and the term "board of directors" when referring to the governing group. Other organizations use other terms, e.g., trustee, governor, board of trustees, board of governors… whatever. The intent is the same.

Here's a question: How do you make these performance expectations work when your board members may be appointed? Sometimes other organizations appoint board members to serve on another organization's board. Sometimes it feels like the board doesn't have much say in who the appointing body appoints. (Or else the board receiving the appointees feels like it doesn't have any control—and when you feel that way, you often behave that way!)

But that perceived lack of control needn't be true—at least not without a big effort to the contrary. In my experience, with careful negotiations and good communications, a board can have significant input into the choices made by the appointing body.

Here's what I mean:

If some other body appoints board members to your board, talk with the appointing body. Explain the importance of performance expectations to produce effective boards. Explain that all board members—whether appointed or elected by the board itself—must be treated the same. Talk about common expectations and shared accountability.

Clearly explain—and carefully negotiate—the importance of the right skills and behaviors to effectively serve as a board member. Describe the professional and intentional process that your board goes through annually to identify the necessary skills and behaviors to best meet community needs.

Encourage the appointing body to welcome your input about the necessary skills and behaviors for candidates. Negotiate carefully, and the appointing body may well allow you to suggest candidates and the reasons why they would be good appointees.

By the way, never forget that the duty of loyalty and allegiance of a board member belongs to the board that member serves on, not to the body that made the appointment.

I believe that all performance expectations apply to all board members… the same performance expectations for each board member. No exceptions. Equity in expectation. Equity in adherence. Equity in enforcement. Equity in consequences.

The last expectation in my board member performance document states: "Agree to step down if unable to fulfill these expectations." Someone suggested that expectation to me when I was teaching somewhere. Brilliant addition. Absolutely brilliant. And an important entrée to firing lousy board members.

Performance Expectations for the Board Member

Each board member of our organization affirms the expectations outlined here and strives to perform accordingly. We treat all board members the same when it comes to these expectations.

We clearly articulate these expectations during the recruitment process. We accept the candidate as a nominee or appointee only after the proposed board member has agreed to fulfill these expectations. And by accepting nomination or appointment, an individual is confirming that this board service is one of that person's top volunteer and giving commitments.

Specific performance expectations are:

1. Believe in and be an active advocate and ambassador for the values, mission, and vision of the organization.

2. Act in a way that contributes to the effective operation of the board— and work with fellow board members and staff to ensure that the board functions well. This includes but is not limited to the following:

    a. Focus on the good of the organization, independent of personal agenda, self-interest, or influence of others.

    b. Support the organization's policies and procedures for conducting business.

    c. Maintain confidentiality of committee, board, and organization work unless authorized otherwise.

    d. Support board decisions once these are made.

    e. Participate in professional development opportunities to strengthen corporate governance and advance the organization's effectiveness through learning. Participate in appraisal of own performance and the performance of the board and its committees.

3. Regularly attend board and committee meetings. Prepare for these meetings by reviewing materials and bringing the materials to meetings. Use conversation as a core business practice, asking strategic questions and participating in dialogue.

4. Keep informed about the organization, its issues, and its connection to the community through active participation within the organization and outreach outside the organization. (Another way of saying this might be: Participate in opportunities to engage in/understand the organization's mission.)

5. Help support the charitable contributions operation of the organization. Specifically, do the following:

   a. Reach into diverse communities and help identify and cultivate relationships to support the organization as donors, volunteers, and advocates.

   b. Give an annual financial contribution to the best of your personal ability. If the organization launches a special campaign, give to that too.

   c. Participate in fund development by taking on various tasks tailored to your comfort and skills.

6. As appropriate, use personal and professional contacts and expertise to benefit the organization without compromising ethics or trespassing on relationships.

7. Be available to serve as a committee/task force chair or member. Be a prepared and active participant.

8. Inform the board of directors of any potential conflicts of interest, whether real or perceived, and abide by the decision of the board related to the situation.

9. Respect the authority of the chief executive officer and staff, and adhere to the limitations of the board, its committees, and individual board members.

10. Agree to step down from your board position if unable to fulfill these expectations.

Notes:

◆ Thanks to Cohort 20, Saint Mary's University master's degree in philanthropy and development for suggesting item 2e.

◆ For item 5b, some organizations make this type of statement: "Consider this organization one of your top two or three charitable commitments."

◆ Item 6 means that each candidate is invited to join the board in order to provide specific expertise to the governance process. The individual is informed of this need—and agrees—prior to nomination or appointment.

principle

PS: The Board and the Individual Board Member

Obviously, the board is made up of individuals. The individual's voice is important within the group. Expect respectful candor from your board members. Remind them that silence is consent—and is unacceptable.

But in the end, for the purposes of governance, the board displays unity of voice. Once individual board members express their perspectives, share their thoughts, argue through disagreements... Once all that is done, the board makes a decision, usually by voting. The board does not seek unanimity. Unanimity is neither necessary nor desirable.

Once the voting is done—and the decision is made—the board displays unity. The decision made is the decision of the group, despite previous disagreement and split votes. The board is a single entity—and its individual board members express that unity.

Confusion and Clarification

So much confusion. So little clarification. As a consultant, I collect lots of examples of the confusion between the board and the board member... and lots of examples of the confusion between governance and management.

Review these examples to test your board and board member understanding.

Part One: The Board and the Board Member

Activity	Board Work	Individual Board Member Work
Raise money to support mission.		X
Support the mission.		X
Make appropriate decisions to ensure sustainability.	X	
Serve as responsible steward for community investment.	X	
Promote a positive image of the organization.		X
Ensure that the organization is healthy and effective.	X	
Identify problems, opportunities, and courses of action.	X	
Recruit board members.	X	

Part Two: Governance or Management		
Activity	Governance	Management
Develop and deliver programs.		X
Ensure appropriate information for strategic conversation.		X
Analyze and research issues.		X
Approve copy for publication, e.g., annual report, newsletter, etc.		X
Ensure that the organization is healthy and effective.	X	X
Define staffing needs.		X
Evaluate board member performance.	X	X
Define policy.	X	X

PPS: Strengthening Your Board

Strengthening your board is an ongoing process. It's easy to take a wrong turn. It's easy to get diverted into micromanagement. It's easy to forget (or disregard) the distinction between the board member and the board itself. It's just plain easy to get distracted!

One rogue board member, a couple of lousy board members, a bad board chair, a weak CEO ... All these things can trigger a board into a whirlwind of dysfunction.

It takes effort from all of you to strengthen the board, to enhance board operations. Here are some tips you can carry out. Your board is doing good work when it does items one through five—and more stuff like this:

1. Adopt conversation as a core business practice. See handout in the Free Download Library at simonejoyaux.com.

2. Use conversation to explore some of the questions in "Building an Effective Board," located in the Free Download Library at simonejoyaux.com.

3. Select blogs in "Simone Uncensored" and talk about what they mean, how your board compares, and what enhancements you all might want to make. In particular, check out the blog category that focuses on boards.

4. Conduct the governance self-assessment posted in the Free Download Library at simonejoyaux.com. Tabulate and analyze the responses. Use the governance committee to lead the board process that makes the necessary improvements.

5. Explore the concept of an executive committee. Don't have one just because other organizations do. Use my antiexecutive committee writings to stimulate conversation within your board. And remember! The board decides if it wants an executive committee or not. The board chair does not decide. The governance committee does not decide. The board decides. And the board decides by using conversation as a core business practice.

To Recap

◆ There's a difference between the board and the individual board member.

◆ There's a difference between governance and management.

◆ Everyone in the organization must understand the distinctions—and behave accordingly.

◆ The best organizations—and you want that to include yours!—adopt and enforce these distinctions.

Chapter Six

Finding the Right Board Members

IN THIS CHAPTER

···→ Composition of the board

···→ Diversity, skills, and behaviors

···→ Identifying candidates

···→ The screening interview

You wouldn't hire a staff person without explaining the job and performance expectations in advance. The same holds true for recruiting board members.

As noted in the previous chapter, your board must adopt a board job description and performance expectations common to all board members. These two policies form the foundation of all subsequent governance work. These policies help you identify, screen, and recruit the right board members for your organization. These two policies help you orient and develop board members. And these two policies help you ensure and enforce the work of the board and the performance of the board members.

But policies don't just spring forth, full born. Like any important decision, conversation is essential to explore ideas, question assumptions, challenge the status quo.

Here's the bad way to develop any policy, including these special two! Quickly suggest the idea without explaining why these policies matter and what value these policies might add. Immediately share drafts without any conversation. And then wait for the confusion, defensiveness, assertion that "everyone knows this stuff." Just watch it all unravel—very quickly!

Before developing these policies—or any others—talk. Conversation is how we learn and change. Through conversation, we listen and question assumptions. Through conversation, we hear and identify key issues and ideas.

Opinion or Expertise?

Refer back to "opinion or expertise" in Chapter Three," Serving on a board is serious business." Does everyone in your organization understand this distinction—and behave accordingly?

principle

During conversation, remember that the body of knowledge "wins." Basic principles and good practice matter. Unqualified personal opinion—without the body of knowledge—just doesn't count.

But don't pound the table—not yet. Don't assert expertise without explanation. Facilitate well. In fact, the enabling functions mentioned earlier—and described more in **Chapter Seven**, "Helping Board and Board Members Succeed"—are essential to secure understanding of and commitment to decisions, including policies defining the board's role and expectations of the board members.

With shared understanding in place—and policies defined—it's easier to identify candidates that bring the right behaviors and skills to the table. Be intentional. This identification process is one of the most important things board members and staff do to help develop an effective board.

Intentionally Composing the Board

I've said it before—and I'll say it again: this whole board thing is serious business.

Don't start thinking about board members until you've thought about the optimum composition of the board:

◆ In order to carry out the role of the board, what skills do you need within the group that is the board?

◆ To work effectively as a group, what behaviors are necessary? (And which behaviors do you intend to avoid?)

◆ To ensure the necessary strategic and critical thinking, inquisitiveness and adaptive capacity to facilitate good governance and due diligence, what diversity is necessary?

In order to do its work effectively, with the highest degree of knowledge and competency, the board must intentionally design its membership to include specific knowledge, skills, experience, and behaviors. All this will be brought together with due consideration for diversity/pluralism.

Board composition is so important that I want a policy. I want the conversation necessary to create good policy. And I want the written, board-approved policy—because policy has to be enforced. Everyone must follow policy. That's what policy means. Competent boards don't tolerate noncompliance.

Any candidate for board membership—whether through nomination and election or appointment—is evaluated through the board composition policy. Here are the kinds of statements that I expect in that composition policy:

1. Knowledge, skills, and experience

   a. Annually, the governance committee identifies the knowledge, skills, and experience necessary to fulfill the legal and moral responsibilities of governance, the organization's values and mission, and current organizational needs.

   b. Knowledge, skills, and experience include but are not limited to financial management, legal, fund development, governance, human resources (e.g., personnel management, conflict resolution, etc.), public relations/marketing, and expertise in the topic of the organization (e.g., human service, environment, health, education, etc.).

   c. Appropriate behaviors are also critical to an effective board. The performance expectations of the individual board member—adopted as policy—summarize the behaviors this organization expects.

2. Gap analysis of current board

   a. The governance committee conducts a gap analysis. The committee evaluates the incumbent board members, determining which knowledge, skills, and experience are currently present within the board and which ones are absent.

   b. The governance committee talks with the full board about the optimum board composition, the results of the gap analysis, and the recommended priorities. The missing knowledge, skills, and experience guide the identification of candidates for this election cycle.

   c. The governance committee also analyzes current board members with due consideration to diversity and networks. Diversity includes but is not limited to gender, ethnicity/race, age, socioeconomics, faith, sexual orientation, etc. Networks include but are not limited to business, social, government, civic, professional, etc.

   d. The governance committee also evaluates the performance of every single board member, determining whether to renominate those with expiring terms or enhance attrition/thank and release nonperformers in the midst of their terms. (Ah, yes, this is the firing-lousy-board-members part!)

3. Identifying qualified candidates in response to the gap analysis

   a. The governance committee helps board members and staff use diversity and network screens (also called a "lens") to identify candidates with the necessary knowledge, skills, and experience.

   b. The governance committee finalizes a preliminary list of candidates for initial outreach. The board reviews, edits as needed, and endorses the preliminary list. The governance committee then conducts screening interviews.

4. Nomination and election

   a. The governance committee finalizes its selection of candidates for nomination and election to the board. Prior to nomination or appointment, each candidate must commit to the organization's values, mission, and policies (particularly those related to the board and individual board members).

b. The governance committee prepares the slate of board members and officers for election to the board. And, of course, there is a screening interview for officers too.

Diversity Lens, Behaviors, and Skills

Pay attention to diversity and pluralism—from gender to generation, sexual orientation to socioeconomics, race/ethnicity to networks. Diversity—experiencing life differently—offers important perspectives and different thinking that is very useful to the deliberations of a board.

Because the board is a group, make sure you're recruiting for behaviors conducive to group process. Here's what I think—and include in my own policy defining board member performance expectations:

In summary, each board member is expected to act in ways that contribute to group effectiveness. Board members are expected to work with each other and the staff to ensure that the board works well.

Specifically, each board member is expected to do the following:

Board Composition Policy

Include concepts and statements like these in your board composition policy.

practical
tip

◆ Focus on the good of the organization, disregarding personal agenda, self-interest, and the influence of others.

◆ Support the organization's policies and procedures for conducting business.

◆ Maintain confidentiality of committee, board, and organization work unless otherwise authorized.

◆ Support decisions once made.

◆ Participate in professional development opportunities to strengthen the organization.

◆ Participate in performance appraisals—one's own individual performance, the board's performance as a group, and the performance of the CEO.

Of course, board members must behave respectfully. Board members must speak candidly. Board members must recognize that silence is consent—and unacceptable in any group process.

Useful Tool

Review **Appendix B**, "Tool to Analyze Board Composition." How would you modify this tool?

👍 practical tip

Your board talks about all this to create shared understanding and group norms. Your board talks about all this to establish policies— and enforce them! What would you add? What would you change? What will your policy include?

Remember: the board talks about why these policies matter. The board explores why a policy is needed—and how it adds value. The board talks about how to manage policies—and how to enforce them.

Identifying Candidates for Board Membership

Okay. Now it's time to move into the annual election cycle.

The governance committee reviews the organization's policy that describes the desired board composition. The governance committee reviews the current composition of the board.

The committee explains its scope of work to the board. The committee reviews the recruitment process, including the why and how of relevant policies and procedures. The committee presents its analysis of skill needs and diversity and network screens.

Then the governance committee facilitates conversation with the board. The committee invites board member comments and questions. The committee encourages suggestions of candidates that meet the organization's needs.

Keep this in mind: first there are candidates. After the screening process, the governance committee produces a slate of nominees.

Keep this in mind too: name names based on needed skills and diversity and network screens. Anyone who suggests any candidate must link that candidate to the skill needs and screens.

Here's another very important angle: use referral sources. A referral source is someone you trust and respect. Ask the referral source to suggest possible candidates who demonstrate the behaviors, skills, diversity, and networks that your organization needs.

And—most importantly—make sure the referral source has direct experience with any suggested candidates. Make sure that referral source Bob actually has worked with suggested candidate Mary. Bob is your insight into how Mary works with others, the value of her insights, the level of her skills, and so forth.

Using referral sources will extend your reach beyond those currently on your board. This important angle can bring in new perspectives and new connections.

But you have to be courageous. You may end up screening candidates that no one in the organization knows. That's okay! You trust and respect your referral source. You test the candidate in your screening interview. Take the risk. Interview. And if the match seems good, nominate and elect.

Conducting the Screening Interview

Your screening interview is as formal and detailed as any job interview. Conduct the interview in a way that allows you to *not* invite the candidate to serve on the board. You don't promise a paid job to an employment candidate when you first begin the interview.

At a screening interview, you ask candidates about the person's experiences and expertise. You invite their questions—and can learn a whole lot about them based on the quality of questions they ask you!

If you get to the point where you are sure you want an individual to serve on your board, then you clearly communicate the role of the board and performance expectations of the individual board member. Do this well!

And always secure commitment to fulfill performance expectations prior to nomination.

So now is the time to set up those screening interviews. Keep in mind, your organization isn't the only doing the screening. The smart candidate is screening you!

First, I don't ever say to someone, "Hi Cynthia. Can you and I meet so I can talk with you about joining our board?" Even if the governance committee considers Cynthia a top candidate, I'm very careful about overpromising.

Here's what I generally say to someone you're pretty darn sure you want on your board: "Hello, Cynthia (gracious social chatter). I'm on the board of Equal Justice for All. We regularly reach out to individuals we think share our values and mission to see about possible engagement opportunities at some point.

"First, let me assure you, I'm not calling for a financial contribution. But I wonder if you might like to meet and explore opportunities.

"Equal Justice regularly seeks people for short-term and long-term projects, one-off activities, committee and board positions, etc. I would welcome the opportunity to meet with you about various opportunities to see if this would be a good match."

Okay. Okay. If lots of us know Cynthia... and we've had good experience with her... and she's even served on one of our committees already... and she has lots of board experience... Then I may well say, "I would welcome the opportunity to meet with you and see if a board or committee position would work for both you and Equal Justice."

But I am very careful not to say, "Hey, Cyn, we want you to join our board. Let's talk, okay?"

You just never know what you might find out during the interview. And you've already kind of offered the position. Now how will extricate yourself when you have second thoughts during the interview?

Now consider the referral situation. No one in your organization knows the individual suggested by that great and trusted referral source. (Let's pretend Sarah Jones is the great referral source who suggested Steve as a possible viable candidate.)

You want to meet with Steve. It would be great if Sarah would send an introductory email to Steve. Of course, you have to work with Sarah on the email. You don't want her saying to Steve: "Hey, buddy, I recommended you as a board member to Equal Justice for All. Simone Joyaux will call you."

Here's what I'd say to Steve: "Hello Steve. My name is Simone Joyaux. Our mutual colleague Sarah Jones referred me to you. I serve on the board of Equal Justice for All.

"First, please let me assure you that I'm not calling to ask you for a gift. Equal Justice regularly reaches out to people in the community to broaden our relationships, develop connections, and get insights and feedback.

"I'm not sure if you know about us. But I would welcome the opportunity to introduce Equal Justice to you and to pick your brain a bit. May I buy you a cup of coffee?"

Yes, This Is Lots of Work!

Finding the right board members is not work for the faint of heart. That's why the governance committee is so important. That's why you need courageous people who have the guts to ask the tough questions and will invest sufficient time doing this work.

Will your organizational culture understand the value of this approach? Will your board members and staff value outreach to those you do not know—yet? Will your screening interviews be so good that you'll actually decide *not* to nominate a candidate?

To Recap

◆ Create a board composition policy and follow it.

◆ Identify candidates with the knowledge, skills, and experience your organization needs.

◆ Use diversity screens/lens to help build the best board.

◆ Don't blow off the screening interview. Don't minimize its importance. Prepare in advance. Draft your questions. Practice with your interview partner(s). Do it right!

◆ Devote enough time to do this work well.

Chapter Seven

Helping the Board and Board Members Succeed

IN THIS CHAPTER

····➜ Activities that help produce success

····➜ Introduction to nineteen enabling functions

····➜ Look in the mirror to make sure you're doing what it takes for your board and board members to succeed

Let's start easy.

Yes, you can launch some practical and easy-to-do activities to help your board and board members succeed. For example:

1. Conduct a comprehensive orientation process for newly elected board members. Provide a "notebook" (print, electronic, intranet, whatever works for your organization) that includes things like: Policies. Previous year's audit. Current year's budget and a couple of current financial reports. Copies of a few board meeting agendas and minutes. Overview of program. Strategic plan. Etc. Give people a chance to read this prior to the orientation. Then host the orientation and invite questions.

2. Some organizations assign mentors to new board members. Mentor and mentee may sit beside each other. Mentor may

contact mentee before and after board meetings to probe for questions and comfort.

3. Regularly offer skills development for board members. How about a few brown-bag lunches focused on topics like: Understanding financial statements. Defining donor-centered fundraising. Tips for relationship building with donors.

4. Host an annual board retreat to explore a particular topic; review the strategic plan; etc.

5. Always set the context for conversations at board meetings by reminding board members of policies and procedures, systems, and processes.

6. Provide background information for each topic on the board meeting agenda. And provide board meeting material to all board members at least seven days prior to the meeting. Give your board members the chance to review the material and come prepared. (And, by the way, never ever provide extra copies of material that has been previously distributed. Hold people accountable! "We sent it to you. You're supposed to read it and bring it." If a board member forgets the material, that board member can find someone to share with.)

Those are the easy things to do. And pretty darn essential too. I've used all these activities as a development officer, board chair, and committee chair. I help my clients develop and use these activities. Yes, they work. You can do it too. If you already do lots of these things, figure out how to enhance them a bit. And invent a few things. In fact, ask your board members what they need from you to help them succeed.

Horses and Water

Remember that staff enables the board, board committees, and individual board members to do the right work well. Staff does this regularly and forever. Actually, good bosses do the same thing with staff: enable people to succeed.

I introduced you to the concept of enabling functions in **Chapter Two**, "Who Is 'You'? Is It 'Me' or Someone Else?" Now read about the horses and water. Can you get into this?

You know the saying: You can lead a horse to water but you cannot make it drink.

I use this tale to create a vision of enabling. So here goes.

The horse in this tale represents a board member. The organization has a herd of horses. They are mostly delightful horses.

There's a wide diversity of horses in the herd because the organization is committed to pluralism. Stallions. Mares. A few colts. Appaloosas. Clydesdales. Arabians and Pintos. Some Shetland ponies too.

Then there is the CEO. The CEO is the principal enabler of the herd. Happily, the CEO is supported by other good enablers on staff.

> Every organization needs highly effective enablers to help get the right stuff done in the right way.
>
> **principle**

They're really good enablers, these people. They looked in the mirror and evaluated and improved their enabling capacity. Don't think whips. Don't think corrals with prickly fences and little shade. Nope. These good enablers have lots of apples and carrots and other highly effective tools. These good enablers have all the right stuff.

Together, the herd of horses and the staff head to the river.

Ah, the river. A glorious place where the horses are happy and frisky and win lots of awards.

But sometimes the way to the river can be troublesome. Actually, the way to the river pretty much always requires effort and skill, slow plodding followed by rushing gallops.

Sometimes there's mud and pebbles along the way. Sometimes overhanging branches scratch the horses. Manes and tails tangle with briars.

But the herd gets to the river because of the leadership, guidance, support, and empowerment by the great enablers.

The great enablers push away the rocks in the path. Then these enablers lift up the horse hooves and remove the uncomfortable pebbles. The great enablers pat the horses and whistle encouragingly.

These enablers offer carrots and bits of apple along the way. And (thanks to an attendee at one of my workshops) sometimes the enablers offer a bit of salt to make sure that the horses are adequately thirsty when they arrive at the river. Also (thanks to another attendee), the enablers clean up the "waste" along the path, as necessary.

The enablers brush horse coats, braid manes and tails. The enablers follow the herd as it takes a bit of a detour to munch on the grass and ruminate.

Sure, sometimes the wind churns the far-away river a bit. That scares some of the horses, and they whinny and balk. But the herd gets through with those good enablers.

Finally, we're at the river.

Our great enablers make sure everyone has a place on the river. Mindful of the old adage, "You can lead a horse to water but you can't make it drink," our enablers kneel down and fill their hands with water. Our great enablers bring their water-filled hands up to the horses' mouths...

And then... if the horse doesn't drink, it's the horse's fault!

The enablers did all they could. These enablers led the horses to water. These enablers made sure that each horse had a place on the river. And these enablers brought water up to the horse's mouth.

Now that darn horse is accountable if it doesn't drink!

The enablers must peer into the mirror. Examine themselves. Did they do all they could to get the horse to drink at the great river?

And whoever doesn't drink... cut them out of the herd. Fire them!

Enabling, the Hard Stuff to Do

Good enabling helps the board, its committees, and board members distinguish between management and governance. Good enabling helps direct the board down the right path. Good enabling is the first line of defense against rogue board members.

Enabling is the process of empowering others. Enabling means giving people the wherewithal, opportunity, and adequate power to act. When you empower someone, you distribute and share your own power. Power shared is power multiplied.

Use enabling always—and you avoid many problems. The problems just don't happen because you've enabled so well. Use enabling to intervene when things break down. Enabling can fix problems when they exist. And, of course, problems always exist. That's life.

Enabling depends on reciprocity, relating, and connecting, Enabling encourages participation, shares responsibility and authority, enhances the self-worth of others, and energizes everyone in the organization.

Effective enabling is not a pejorative concept. Good enabling is not patronizing. True enabling is a value-driven philosophy that invests influence and responsibility in all parties. And that's what you need to do good governance and develop leaders. Effective enabling is the primary factor in a healthy relationship between governance and management. Make enabling work, and there's less firing required.

To date, I've defined nineteen enabling functions. In summary, here are my enabling functions. Remember, staff carries out these enabling functions with volunteers, including board members and fundraising volunteers. And supervisors do this with their staff too.

On the following page is the list of all nineteen enabling functions.

But watch out. Follow my blog and other writings. Periodically, I add more, thanks to conversation with colleagues.

Now here are the current nineteen, briefly described:

1. Transmit the organization's values.

   Live your organization's values. Walk the talk. Show your board members (and everyone else) how your organization's values form the foundation and framework for each action.

2. Engage volunteers in the meaning of your organization.

   Tell stories. Share experiences. Have conversations. Engage your volunteers so they feel your cause and mission in their guts.

   Think about all that stuff your board members have to talk about to do governance well. Every board has to talk about the same stuff: money, legal and regulatory compliance, CEO performance, etc.

The Nineteen Enabling Functions

1. Transmit values.

2. Engage volunteers in the meaning of your organization.

3. Articulate expectations and clarify roles and relationships.

4. Respect and use the skills, expertise, experience, and insights of volunteers.

5. Engage volunteers in process as well as tasks.

6. Provide direction and resources. Explain why, not just how. Identify and remove barriers; develop skills.

7. Coach and mentor people to succeed.

8. Transmit the body of knowledge and best practice, helping others anticipate next practice.

9. Communicate and help transform information into knowledge and sharing.

10. Encourage people to question organizational assumptions and personal assumptions and ask strategic and cage-rattling questions.

11. Engage people in meaningful conversation that produces learning and change.

12. Ensure quality decision making.

13. Anticipate conflicts and facilitate resolution.

14. Encourage volunteers to use their power, practice their authority, and accept their responsibility.

15. Model behavior.

16. Manage.

17. Create opportunities/strategies to buy more time to think things through.

18. Enhance attrition (and facilitate thank and release, if necessary).

19. Monitor, evaluate, and enhance enabling.

principle

What happens when board members don't remember why your organization is different from any other organization? What do you do at board meetings to engage board members in the heart and soul of the organization, in the meaning of the cause and the impact of their governance work?

3. Articulate expectations and clarify roles and relationships.

    The best enablers help others understand distinctions and connections, responsibilities and accountabilities... and limitations too. Make sure you think through all of this before you engage anyone.

4. Respect and use the skills, expertise, experience, and insights of volunteers.

    Use me well or leave me alone! Help me use my talents. Encourage me to share my insights and experience. Make sure that I understand the difference between opinion and expertise.

5. Engage volunteers in process as well as tasks.

    When people understand why, it's easier to understand the how and to do the what. Set the context. Explain the background. Show your volunteers (and staff!) how stuff fits together. Don't just assign tasks.

6. Provide direction and resources. Explain why, not just. Identify and remove barriers; develop skills.

    I know you know this is just common sense. So how come we don't carry out this enabling function?

    We assume they know what governance is since they served on so many boards. Okay, I talked about that early in this manual. We assume they know what fundraising is too. Okay, not true.

    And what about barriers? When did you or I last ask any board members what else they were facing that week or month—at home or at work? How clearly did you or I explain how long something was going to take—and what problems to anticipate and overcome?

7. Coach and mentor people to succeed.

   Have you ever felt abandoned in a task? Whether you are staff or board, I hope you know what it's like to operate without a net, without a cheerleading voice, without... well, just without.

8. Transmit the body of knowledge and best practice, helping other anticipate next practice.

   Review "opinion or expertise" in **Chapter Three**, "Serving on a Board Is Serious Business." Make sure your board members know what they need know to do corporate governance, that together thing. Make sure your board members know enough to operate effectively as leadership volunteers outside board meetings. But do remember, your board members don't need to know as much as the staff does.

9. Communicate and help transform information into knowledge and learning.

   Your board members need to know enough to have a strategic conversation. Don't keep secrets. And don't let one group know things that the others don't know. (One of my pet peeves about executive committees.)

   Don't just give people data. Explain the meaning of the data. Highlight the trends. Summarize the implications. Encourage your board members to probe deeply (in the right stuff, not the wrong stuff) to identify additional implications.

10. Encourage people to question organizational and personal assumptions and ask strategic and cage-rattling questions.

    Asking questions isn't disrespectful nor should it be a rebellion. Think about all the questions that you might wish someone or some official body had asked before "all hell broke loose." Maybe it was a war or a housing bubble or an economic crisis or an oil spill or a campus shooting or... Think about all the questions that various boards could—and should— have asked before various debacles in both for-profit and nonprofit organizations.

11. Engage people in meaningful conversation that produces learning and change.

     Conversation happens because people ask questions. Lovely curious questions about someone else's interests. Strategic questions to advance business dialogue. Cage-rattling questions that challenge the status quo and scare people just enough to launch change.

     Human conversation can produce learning and change. Conversation can start revolutions, change entire societies. Read Theodore Zeldin's lovely little book, *Conversation: How Talk Can Change Our Lives.*

12. Ensure quality decision making.

     How many bad decisions have you seen made? How many bad decisions have you made? These enabling functions can help avoid bad decisions—or fix them.

13. Anticipate conflicts and facilitate resolution.

     Disagreement and conflict happen. And that isn't bad. Get over it! With important issues, of course, people disagree. Remember, we don't want the mediocrity consensus coming from the lowest common denominator that we could agree upon.

14. Encourage volunteers to use their power, practice their authority, and accept their responsibility.

     The spreading of power is good. Shared power is good.

     Of course, sometimes hierarchy is essential. Sometimes it's my power and not yours. Or yours and not mine. But not always. Get over this too. Share power.

     And be very clear what isn't your right and is someone else's. That is particularly important in governance and management.

15. Model behavior.

     This is a bit like enabling function 1, transmitting values. Walk the talk. Behave as you want others to behave. You know the drill.

16. Manage.

    Someone has to manage the situations, the organization, the enabling functions. And I know, for sure, that it isn't me, the volunteer.

    I'm a board member. I participate in governance. You don't want me to intrude in management. So manage this stuff yourself!

    I'm a board member and a fundraising volunteer (or just a fundraising volunteer). If you don't manage... what happens if I intervene. Oh dear.

17. Create opportunities/strategies to buy more time to think things through.

    This whole enabling thing means balancing all these functions simultaneously. You have to think on your feet and behind your desk. You have to think face to face with that rogue board chair while listening to the committee direct staff, all in the midst of a complicated conversation at a board meeting.

    That's life. Sorry to be so blunt.

    Yet, sometimes, we just can't do it. I'm there in the midst of a small little mess that could morph into a big messy mess. I need some time to figure this out. You're stuck in the middle of a mess that's moving to a morass. Your hands seem to be tied. If only you had a bit of a breather.

    To enable well, we have to find a way, launch a strategy, create a teeny, tiny opportunity to buy more time. "Oh my, look at the time. We will have to continue this conversation later, as I have to fly to Brussels to rescue the eurozone. Let's resume this conversation a bit later."

    "Hmm... Let me take some time to reflect on what you've shared. Then we can start again." "Gosh... Wow... I think I'll do a bit of research on that and reach out to some of my colleagues (and my kitty) to gather more information."

    You get the idea.

18. Enhance attrition (and facilitate thank and release, if necessary).

Well, look at that. Here it is. Enabling function number eighteen is the core of this manual. Yes, fire lousy board members. But you cannot fire anyone until you've effectively executed—and repeatedly tried—all of the preceding seventeen enabling functions.

And once we get here—to the firing—how can there be a nineteenth enabling function? It's pretty obvious:

19. Monitor, evaluate, and enhance enabling.

How are you doing? How would your board appraise your performance of enabling? What's the feedback you get from those you trust? How well does your staff enable each other, their staff, and the volunteers they work with?

What I Learned. How About You?

It's okay if you don't like the word "enabling." Use another word. (I tried but couldn't come up with anything better—and I even asked some twenty highly experienced fundraisers back in 1996 when I first was putting together these thoughts.)

Whatever it's called—and for me it's enabling… That's what I didn't understand back in Lansing, Michigan.

If I had done everything I could back in Lansing… then I could hold them accountable. But I didn't do all that I could possibly do. I didn't even know what to do—or why or how. So how could I do it? And without my leadership—my enabling—how could I hold them accountable?

> ### Enabling
>
> For lots more detail about enabling functions, see *Strategic Fund Development: Building Profitable Relationships That Last*, 3rd ed. What you have here is just the summary, just a taste to move you forward.
>
>  practical tip

Happily, I've learned over the intervening years. I've been articulating the concept of enabling—and adding to it—since 1994 when I first wrote an article in a series called *New Directions for Philanthropic Fundraising.*

How curious. My article was printed in the volume called *Nonprofit Organizational Culture: What Fundraisers Need to Know*. Even then, I hope I realized that this enabling thing is as much about organizational culture as it is about strategy and tactics.

Enabling is what I've learned. It helps with governance and fund development and other things too, I suspect.

For now, look in the mirror. Each of you. Right now. Look in the mirror like I did years after my experience in Lansing. Like I keep trying to do better and better with a client or as a board member chairing a committee.

Yes, look in the mirror.

Are you the chief executive effectively enabling your board members, the board, and its committees? How about the other staff members who work closely with the board and its committees? Does your fundraiser help the fund development committee understand the distinction between governance and management? Does your fundraiser help board members succeed in their leadership role as volunteers outside the board meeting?

How are you doing, leading the horses to water? It's your job, helping board members succeed. Only then do you have the right to talk about firing lousy board members.

To Recap

- ◆ You and I and everyone must help the board and its members succeed. Together, we are accountable.

- ◆ Effective enabling helps the board and board members do the right stuff—and stay away from the other stuff.

- ◆ No matter what you call them, my nineteen enabling functions help you avoid problems—and intervene and fix problems when necessary. I do it. My clients do it. My students do it. Try it.

- ◆ The buck stops with staff. Staff is most accountable for helping volunteers—including board members—succeed.

Chapter Eight

Monitoring Performance

IN THIS CHAPTER

···➔ Who is accountable for this work?

···➔ Role of the governance committee

···➔ What I expect of board members

···➔ Informal and formal monitoring

So now you think you're ready to monitor performance—and some firing?

Not so fast! Reread all the previous chapters. Pay attention to the big concepts and littlest details.

Pay attention to the concept of organizational culture, the beliefs and norms. Sure, it's helpful to have policies and procedures and systems. But without an organizational culture of excellence—commonly accepted norms about expectations and screening and monitoring performance and firing—then the best policies, procedures, and systems won't do you any good.

Always remember: you can't evaluate performance without articulating expectations first. That's why the board job description and the board member performance expectations provide the foundation and framework for firing lousy board members.

Another always: you can't fire someone without comparing the individual's performance with the clearly articulated expectations. You can't fire someone without providing feedback and the opportunity for improvement first.

The board's governance committee does all this, just about every step described here. The board establishes a committee to provide leadership, in partnership with the chief executive. The committee reports to the board. The board talks about stuff and takes action.

The chief executive enables both the board and its governance committee. The chief executive makes sure that all this stuff happens—and happens well.

And every single board member is accountable too. Every single board member pays attention to process. Every single board member participates in process. Every single board member asks questions and challenges assumptions. Every single board member holds herself or himself accountable and demands that the other board members hold themselves equally accountable.

Committee Members

I think all board committees should include non-board members. You can include retired board members on any committee. You can use committee membership as a testing ground for future board member candidates. And there are people who love your organization and want to volunteer but don't want board membership. Those individuals may welcome committee service.

food for thought

Here's another tidbit to remember: many of us consider the governance committee to be the most important board committee. This is the committee that is responsible to help ensure a top-notch board. This committee is not some quick afterthought!

Make sure you appoint a darn good chair, one with guts and attention to process. Make sure that chair is committed to engaging committee members and board members in the process.

Hmm … I just described a good committee chair for any committee!

Make sure the governance committee begins its work at the

start of the board year. The nominations and election process are only one small part of the committee's work. And that portion of the work should begin at least six months prior to the election. Otherwise, how will you identify and screen candidates?

What I Expect of Board Members—And You Should Too

Here's the thing: I want board members who are willing to inconvenience themselves on behalf of the organization. Some examples: Celebrate your life partner's birthday on a different day when the actual birth date is the same date of the board meeting. Attend the board meeting. Miss the Fleetwood Mac (or Justin Bieber) concert because it's a board meeting date. If possible, avoid scheduling a vacation when there's a board meeting. Serve on the fundraising event committee even though you despise events. Do it because your organization said it really needs you this time.

Here's another thing: I don't want board members who are so busy that they cannot attend board meetings regularly. Release the board member whose personal and/or professional life doesn't allow regular board meeting attendance. Now is just not the right time. Use the person on a committee or as a resource. Remember, a person who misses board meetings regularly cannot be considered a good board member.

Formal and Informal Monitoring

Monitoring performance can be informal. For example, as a board chair, I call board members who are absent. I don't care if board member Mary RSVP'd her absence. If she's absent a couple of times, I'm calling to touch base. I find out what's happening. I explain how much we all value her input and participation. I remind her, graciously, of the performance expectations. I keep watch and, if necessary, bring her performance up to the chief executive and the governance committee.

Monitoring performance must be formal too. The governance committee appraises each board member's performance annually—no matter where the board member is in completion of term. The governance committee compares each board member's actual performance with the clearly articulated performance expectations. The governance committee decides if any board member needs feedback.

For example, think about Bob, who is in the second year of his three-year term. The governance committee is concerned about Bob's not-so-

Resources for You

See **Appendixes C** and **D** for two different performance appraisal tools for board members.

practical tip

great performance. A representative of the governance committee talks with Bob, providing feedback and helping Bob identify ways to improve his performance. If Bob doesn't improve, then the governance committee moves into the stages of firing lousy board members. Effective organizations do not let nonperforming board members stick around until their terms expire.

You can also develop a tool and ask board members to assess their own performance. But be careful. This *never* substitutes for evaluation by the governance committee. Self-assessment is just not that effective. Research shows that the weakest performers evaluate themselves positively. Oops.

The Uncomfortable Bylaws Statement

Here's another very important item: the statement that all bylaws should include—but you never want to use it if you can possibly avoid it.

Here's the statement, called "Removal":

"The board may remove any officer or director for cause by two-thirds (2/3) vote of all directors then in office, at any regular or special meeting of the board, provided that a statement of the reason or reasons shall have been mailed by registered mail to the officer or director proposed for removal at least thirty (30) days before any final action is taken by the board. This statement shall be accompanied by a notice of the time when, and the place where, the board is to take action on the removal. The officer or director shall be given an opportunity to be heard and the matter considered by the board at the time and place mentioned in the notice."

Yes, that very uncomfortable statement should be in every organization's bylaws. But you don't want to use it. Nope. Not ever. Avoid it at all costs. Please. Avoid taking such public, in-front-of-everyone action against a board member. In general, don't vote someone off the board.

Imagine how awkward that would be. Imagine how public that would become. Imagine all the discomfort and hurt feelings and anger and embarrassment. Just imagine.

Yes, make sure you have the removal statement. Just in case.

But avoid the "just in case." Instead, use the private "firing lousy board members" process.

To Recap

◆ Everything else has to be in place before you can monitor performance: organizational culture and policies, like the board's job description and performance expectations of board members.

◆ Everyone shares accountability for good performance.

◆ Monitoring performance is an ongoing informal and formal process.

Chapter Nine

The Chicken Way Out

Here's a conversation at the governance committee:

"Well, Bob Smith hasn't been the greatest performer. He misses lots of board meetings and isn't active in his committee assignment either. And when he does attend, we have to repeat all the stuff he missed, which is rather disruptive."

"All true. But he has only one more year to complete his term. Let it go. And we just won't renominate him at the end of this term."

Or how about these remarks from the chief development officer:

"Mary Smith is one of our biggest donors. Removing her from the board might jeopardize that gift. I strongly urge you all to just leave her alone. It's okay to have a few nonperformers on the board. And, anyway, the other board members don't much like fundraising and won't want to have to compensate for the loss of her gift."

And how about this from the CEO:

"Tom Jones is the CEO of the largest bank in this community. We want to get another grant from his bank. And he usually solicits those other three CEOs. We just cannot afford to lose Tom's contacts or annoy him."

Ah, how those chickens just cluck and cluck.

I've heard every one of those conversations as a development officer, executive director, board chair, chair of the governance committee, and chair of the fund development committee. I recognize those conversations are real. But I don't accept them as a guide to good governance. I've seen too much damage when boards acquiesce to those conversations.

I do understand. This is hard work. What do we all expect? This is a business, not a party. This is a business, not a gathering of friends hanging out.

Your Organization's Health

I'll say it again. No individual is more important than the health of the organization. No individual exception adds sufficient value to justify bad governance.

principle

Maybe Bylaws Could Fix the Performance Problem

When it's hard to do something, we often seek work-arounds. We find ways to avoid what we should do.

There's a bylaws statement that is often used as this work-around: "If you miss three consecutive meetings, you're assumed to have resigned." And then the organization sends a letter to the offending board member. Or the organization chickens out and doesn't send the letter.

That bylaws statement (or a policy with that statement) is flawed. Get rid of it.

Here's the reality: I attend one board meeting and then miss two. Then I attend two and miss two. Then I attend two and miss one. But I didn't miss three consecutive meetings! Really? Do you want me on your board? As great as I am—and I'm great—I'm not a good board member if I miss that many meetings.

Don't say, "Well, that board member RSVP'd, so it's an excused absence." I don't care if it's an excused absence. If you miss too many meetings—even if it's for your work—you don't add value to our board. The board is a group, and governance happens only when we are together. Your too-frequent absences make you a bad board member. You're still a great person. And you may support us in other ways. That's great! But it's not working for us to have you serve as a board member.

Don't Be Chicken

Don't use that bylaws statement. Don't succumb to those conversations that started this chapter.

Instead, ask yourself: How do we create a sustainable organization? How do we ensure good governance? How do we engage and retain the best people?

Now ask yourself: How do you think other hard-working board members feel? How much time is spent compensating for these nonperformers? And, hey, what's the word on the street about your governance effectiveness and your resolution of problems?

Bad individual performance is disruptive to good group process. Badly performing board members frustrate and exhaust competent staff and board members.

And bad performance spreads like a virus. Good board members may actually follow the bad role models periodically. Good board members eventually leave.

So don't chicken out. Address the problem. Monitor performance. Provide feedback. And fire those lousy board members before the contagion is widespread.

To Recap

- ◆ The governance committee—as well as its members—is supposed to be tough. Don't chicken out!

- ◆ This is a business. Do it well or suffer the consequences.

- ◆ A bylaws statement doesn't fix the situation.

Chapter Ten

Finally, Feedback Time

IN THIS CHAPTER

···→ Enhance attrition—that's the best way

···→ Thank and release—if attrition doesn't work

···→ Be professional and gracious

The governance committee speaks formally with the board member about performance. No staff person does this! The board chair is not in charge of doing this. This is governance committee work.

A member of the governance committee speaks with the nonperformer. This is a formal conversation, not a casual mini mention. Arrange a time to speak. Explain that the conversation is about the board member's performance and adherence to the agreed-upon expectations. Be clear that you are representing the governance committee and its concerns.

Make this a respectful and gracious conversation. There's no firing, no nastiness. The governance committee representative is providing feedback from the governance committee. The governance committee representative is finding out why the board member is not fulfilling performance expectations.

Remind the board member about the agreed-upon performance expectations. Express concern about the board member's performance compared with the agreed-upon standards. Be specific when expressing the concerns. For example, concerns might include board and committee meeting attendance or disruptive behavior at meetings.

Probe to see what's going on. Be sympathetic and understanding. Yes, the board member might be experiencing personal and professional challenges. While that's a reason, it's not an excuse. Either the board member fixes the performance issues or the personal and professional challenges require resignation. Clearly—and graciously—explain all this.

The governance committee representative is trying to help the nonperformer think through the situation. The nonperforming board member has to commit to improving—and improving now. Talk about what that looks like.

Sometimes there might be two formal conversations providing feedback and asking for change. But, really, only two. Then it's time to end this.

Enhance Attrition

Aim to "enhance attrition" first. The goal is to help board member Sherry recognize that she isn't fulfilling her obligations—and apparently cannot. The goal is to help board member Peter say, "Well, maybe this isn't the best time for me to serve on this board even though I really want to."

Agree with alacrity and say, "It seems best for you to resign at this time due to personal or professional reasons. It happens, you know. It's okay."

You're facilitating a conversation to help someone gain insight. You're helping someone who cares lots about your organization and is just reluctant to let go.

That's "enhancing attrition."

As appropriate, invite the individual to continue with committee service. Attendance at committee meetings is not as stringent as it is at board meetings.

Be clear that you want a written letter or email. Indicate that you will inform the board that the individual is resigning due to personal and professional commitments.

Make sure that the board chair—and the CEO too—sends a personal, gracious, and warm thank-you letter for time served. You want to keep this relationship!

Self-Firing

Let me tell you a colleague's story. Her pseudonym is Jennifer.

"Well, Simone, I finally confronted the board at a board meeting. I was nice. But I was firm. I said to them, 'You should fire me! That's your job when someone isn't performing! But since you haven't done it, I'm firing myself!'

"I had been feeling guilty, Simone, because I was missing so many meetings. My work got out of control. I kept trying to be a good board member, but I knew my performance wasn't good enough.

"When I confronted them, they were shocked. And they started to say things like, 'But you are so good, Jennifer. We need your expertise in governance and fundraising. You're so wonderful at board meetings.'

"'But I'm not making it to board meetings,' I said with some exasperation. 'I like you all. I love this organization. I want to do a good job, but I just cannot. So you have to let me go. I'm firing myself.'"

And then my colleague said to me: "I'm just not sure they understood why they should have fired me. I even kinda explained the concept of enhancing attrition to them. I'm still not sure they got it.

"But I hope that my action will make them think. I hope my self-firing will force them to pay more attention and not get seduced by an oh-so-cool board member. I hope my self-firing will empower them to launch an attrition-enhancing/thank-and-release program."

> Wow. Self-firing would be the best. But it's very unusual. Aim for attrition. And, if necessary, thank the board member and demand resignation. Graciously, of course.
>
> **food for thought**

Jennifer felt guilty. In my experience, a significant number of nonperforming board members suspect that they are failing. These board members already feel guilty. These board members recognize that they are not fulfilling the obligations they made. Your job is to help them along the departure path, the attrition road.

Thank and Release

Thank and release is more assertive—more aggressive—than enhancing attrition. I typically urge enhancing attrition first. But if that doesn't work, then move to the next level.

If there's no change, after one formal feedback conversation and the promise to do better… Then it's probably time for thank and release. The organization tried to enhance attrition. But the board member didn't resign. And then the board member didn't improve performance.

Now it's time to graciously and kindly say to that nonperforming board member: "You need to step down. Please resign because you cannot fulfill what you agreed to do." That's "thank and release."

Do thank and release graciously too. Don't embarrass anyone. Build on the previous conversations you've had—when you provided feedback and explained the necessary improvements. Remind the board member of the agreed-upon performance expectations. Explain that you will report this as a resignation due to personal and professional obligations.

I've done thank and release via a formal letter. The person wasn't returning calls. But, I certainly wouldn't thank and release via email.

Be as kind and caring as possible. Be sympathetic and understanding.

But do it. This is a professional relationship.

Remember **Chapter Three**, "Serving on a Board Is Serious Business." That's the truth. This is serious business. This is business, not personal. This is professional, not social.

I always wince when I hear staff or board members tell me "we're all friends." This is a business situation. Yes, you want to be cordial. Yes, maybe a couple of board members are friends.

Nonetheless, when we're doing board work and talking about the sustainability of the organization, this is a business. This is a professional relationship.

Maybe that's something you should think about when you recruit board members. Avoid family and friends—unless the candidates tell you they can separate business and friendship when necessary. Ask that question. Pursue that issue in conversation.

Make very sure everyone understands that this is a business activity and a business relationship and a professional situation. Do the right stuff first, no matter how difficult. Do the right stuff first—so the really hard right stuff is not quite so hard later.

To Recap

◆ Provide feedback about a board member's performance.

◆ Be respectful and gracious and professional.

◆ Deal with inadequate performance and poor performers. Yes, that means "fire them."

Conclusion

This Sure Takes a Long Time!

Yes, indeed.

This work takes a long time. It's a process—over time. It's not "fire now."

And it isn't easy.

But it isn't as hard as organizations (and people) think it is.

It is not acceptable to keep nonperformers around. Nonperformers demotivate and frustrate hard workers. Nonperformers waste valuable staff and board time.

Your unwillingness to deal with nonperformers sends a very bad message to others.

This is serious business. You deserve better. Everyone does. So go for it. Get it together.

But...

I know. You have "buts." Talk about them. Explore them. That's part of getting it together.

This is scary and worrisome. What if the person gets mad and badmouths you? Make sure you do this graciously and carefully.

By the way, explain to me exactly how bad performers will badmouth you. "The organization asked me to resign because I wasn't performing well." Hmm... "The organization asked me to resign because I was so brilliant and insightful and I threatened them all."

Yes, I know, the fired person could maybe say something awful. So? If Mr. Jones is so awful that he would actually badmouth your organization—isn't he too awful to stay on your board?

You think it's hard to find board members and don't want to lose any. Hey! Your organization deserves high-performing board members. Don't accept less. Yes, there are more candidates out there. Look harder. Reach into new networks. Use referral sources effectively. Spend more time finding the right candidates and screening them well.

Firing Lousy Board Members ... And Helping the Others Succeed

Lots of your board members saved themselves already. They do a fine job pretty much on their own.

Some board members need help. Then they'll be fine too. It's your job to save them.

And which "you" does the saving? All five of the "yous:" You, the organization, and your culture and systems. You, the CEO, with your great enabling. You, the board, ensuring that you are fulfilling the governance responsibility related to the board and board members. You, all the other good individual board members who model appropriate behavior and fight against bad behavior. And you, the governance committee, assiduously carrying out your scope of work.

And a few—not all that many, hopefully—need to leave. Now. You just have to fire them!

And Finally

This is actually *not* about firing lousy board members. This is about enhancing attrition. You work hard to avoid thank and release. And you never use the word "fire." And, of course, you don't use the word "lousy."

And just maybe this manual isn't even about firing lousy board members. Maybe this manual is really about finding and nurturing and keeping the right board members so they can do the right stuff in the right way so your organization can be ever stronger and better meet the needs of those in need, thus creating a stronger community and better world.

Whew. How was that?

Everyone is accountable. You are accountable, and so am I. The board chair is accountable, and so is the CEO. And every single board member is accountable too.

Each of us models good behavior and bad behavior too. Each of us demonstrates the willingness to be inconvenienced—or not. Together we make this work—or together we fail.

But now I'm thinking of something new. I'm thinking about impact: the impact that you or I might have as an individual board member. The impact that we board members together—as the board—might have.

I'm not thinking about a board member performing well, fulfilling the expectations. I'm not thinking about the board performing well, fulfilling the job description of the board.

I'm thinking about something greater. I'm not sure I know how to express this well yet. But here goes.

As an individual board member, did I have a meaningful impact on the board and on the organization? For example, did my fellow board members see me as a positive example—even an inspiring example? Did my behavior help model for others the way to do our shared work effectively? Did my strategic questions appropriately (and without threat) help others question their own assumptions? Did I welcome challenges from others, honestly querying myself? Did my insights and observations help generate conversation and learning?

And what about us as a board? Together, did we produce meaningful impact for this organization and for our community? Will we be remembered well?

Appendix A

Adapted from various resources by Simone P. Joyaux, ACFRE, simonejoyaux. com. (See Joyaux website for performance appraisal information for CEO as well as job description for chief development officer.)

Job Description for the Chief Executive Officer

Position title: various terms, e.g., executive director, managing director, CEO, etc.

Reports to: board of directors

Reporting to this position: depends upon the organization

Job Summary

The chief executive, in partnership with the board, is responsible for the success of this organization. Together, the board and CEO ensure the organization's relevance to the community, accountability to its diverse constituencies, and accomplishment of impact and results.

The board delegates responsibility for management and day-to-day operations to its chief executive, who has the authority to carry out these responsibilities in accordance with the direction and policies established by the board.

Accountabilities

1. Legal and regulatory compliance

   Ensures the filing of all legal and regulatory documents and monitors compliance with relevant laws and regulations.

2. Mission, policy, and planning

   a. Provides leadership to the board to determine the organization's values, mission, vision, and short- and long-term goals.

   b. Provides leadership to help the board monitor and evaluate the organization's relevancy to the community and the organization's effectiveness, impact, and results.

   c. Keeps the board fully informed on the organization's health and effectiveness and on all the important factors influencing the organization:

      ◆ Identifies problems and opportunities and addresses them, brings those that are appropriate to the board and/or its committees, and facilitates discussion and deliberation.

      ◆ Informs the board and its committees about trends, issues, problems, and activities in order to facilitate policy making. Recommends policy positions.

   d. Keeps informed of developments in the organization's area of work as well as in nonprofit management and governance, and philanthropy and fund development.

   e. Ensures that the appropriate policies are in place to guide the organization's work in all areas.

3. Management and administration

   a. Provides general oversight of all the organization's activities, manages the day-to-day operations, holds staff accountable while directing and delegating the day-to-day operations, and ensures a smoothly functioning, efficient, and effective organization.

   b. Ensures program quality and organizational stability through development and implementation of standards and controls, systems and procedures, and regular evaluation.

    c. Ensures a work environment that recruits, retains, and supports quality staff and volunteers. Ensures process for selecting, developing, motivating, and evaluating staff and volunteers.

    d. Recommends staffing, staff compensation, and financing to the board of directors. In accordance with board action, recruits personnel, negotiates professional contracts, and sees that appropriate salary structures are developed and maintained.

    e. Specifies accountabilities for management personnel (whether paid or volunteer), ensures ongoing feedback, and conducts formal performance appraisal annually.

4. Governance

    a. Serves as the organization's key resource and facilitator for good governance.

    b. Helps the board articulate its own role and accountabilities and those of its committees and individual members; helps evaluate performance regularly.

    c. Works with the board chair to enable the board to fulfill its governance functions and manages the board's due-diligence process to ensure timely attention to core issues.

    d. With the board chair, focuses board attention on long-range strategic issues.

    e. Works with the board officers and committee chairs to get the best thinking and involvement of each board member and to stimulate all board members to give their best.

    f. Recommends volunteers to participate in the board and its committees.

5. Finance

    a. Promotes programs and services that are produced in a cost-effective manner, employing economy while maintaining an acceptable level of quality.

     b. Oversees the fiscal activities of the organization, including budgeting, reporting, and auditing, and ensures adequate controls.

     c. Works with board to ensure financing to support short- and long-term goals.

6. Philanthropy and fund development

     a. Fosters a culture of philanthropy throughout the organization and ensures a donor-centered organization that nurtures loyalty through a comprehensive relationship-building program.

     b. Ensures an effective fund development program by serving as the chief development officer or by hiring and supervising an individual responsible for this activity.

     c. Ensures a comprehensive gift management system, analysis, and reporting to support quality decision making.

     d. Ensures the availability of materials to support solicitation.

     e. Provides leadership in developing and implementing the organization's fundraising plan and monitoring the plan's progress.

     f. Helps ensure that board members carry out philanthropy and fund development activities.

     g. Participates actively in identifying, cultivating, and soliciting donor prospects.

7. Relationship building

     a. Facilitates the process of identifying the key relationships necessary to support an effective organization and ensures proper planning, relationship building, and communications to develop and maintain these.

     b. Facilitates the integration of the organization into the fabric of the community by ensuring the use of effective marketing and communications activities.

c. Acts as an advocate, within the public and private sectors, for issues relevant to the organization, its services, and constituencies.

d. Listens to clients, staff, volunteers, donors, and the community in order to improve services and generate community involvement. Ensures awareness of the organization's response to community needs by the organization's diverse constituencies.

e. Serves as the organization's chief spokesperson, ensuring proper representation of the organization to the community.

f. Works with legislators, regulatory agencies, volunteers, and representatives of the nonprofit sector to promote legislative and regulatory policies that encourage a healthy community and address the issues of the organization's constituencies.

Working Conditions

This is a senior position holding full responsibility for the organization's operations. Handles detailed, complex concepts and problems, balances multiple tasks simultaneously, and makes rapid decisions regarding administrative issues.

Plans and implements programs. Establishes strong and appropriate relationships with the board, committees, volunteers, staff, donors, and clients. Develops smooth and constructive relationships with executive colleagues, outside agencies, organizations, and individuals.

Plans and meets deadlines. Maintains a flexible work schedule to meet the demands of executive management. Hours may be long and irregular.

Conveys a professional and positive image and attitude regarding the organization and the nonprofit sector. Demonstrates commitment to continued professional growth and development.

Is a decisive individual who possesses a big-picture perspective and is well versed in systems.

Qualifications

A bachelor's degree is required, with a minimum of five years' experience in a senior management position. As chief executive officer, this individual demonstrates critical competencies in four broad categories: commitment to results, business savvy, leading change, and motivating.

Commitment to Results

The CEO is a systems thinker who is customer focused and goal driven. This individual identifies relevant information and helps transform this information into individual and organizational knowledge and learning. The chief executive is action oriented and innovative. The CEO translates broad goals into achievable steps. The CEO anticipates and solves problems and takes advantage of opportunities and is a self-starter and team player.

Business Savvy

As the organization's leader, this position requires an individual with knowledge of and experience in management and administration. The position requires demonstrated experience in integrating and coordinating diverse areas of management:

◆ Knowledge required in general business management and leadership.

◆ Some experience in the nonprofit sector, corporate governance, and philanthropy and fund development is preferred. If the candidate does not have this experience at the time of hiring, the candidate is expected to study and develop these knowledge areas in a timely fashion.

◆ A high level of personal skills and comfort with diversity is required to deal effectively with people from all segments of the community.

◆ Must be able to effectively communicate orally and in writing.

◆ Must be an excellent negotiator.

Leading Change

The chief executive possesses the skills and implements the functions of a leader. The CEO shares the organization's values, mission, and vision. The CEO consistently displays integrity, models behavior, develops people, and builds productive teams. This individual deals effectively with demanding situations and designs and implements interventions. The CEO leads the continuous improvement effort.

Motivating

The chief executive manages continuity, change, and transition. This individual knows how to influence and enable others. The CEO addresses the impact of attitude and action on the organization and its participants.

Appendix B

Tool to Analyze Board Composition

This inventory tool is based on the board composition policy. The grid is reviewed annually and adjusted as necessary. Individuals are recruited for particular skills—in partnership with the use of diversity and network screens.

Knowledge, Skills, Experience. Diversity and Networks. Behaviors.

The optimum candidates for board membership reflect the behaviors your organization expects, plus bring particular skills into the boardroom that assist with governance and reflect the diversity and networks that are important to your organization.

Board Member Name	Knowledge/Skills/Experience												
	Legal Expertise	Finance: Budget, Oversight	Finance: Investment	Strategic Planning	Fund Development: Body of Knowledge	Human Resources	Business Management	Governance	Mission Expertise	Marketing/ Communications	Nonprofit Management	What Else Would You Add?	Generalist*
1.													
2.													
3.													
4.													
5.													
6.													
7.													
8.													
9.													
10.													
11.													
12.													
Etc.													

*Does "generalist" make sense? Add value? Or is this an attempt to create a category for individuals who do not bring something else to the table?

Without the right behaviors, knowledge, skills, and experience are pretty much useless.

Consider the behaviors listed on the following page. You can, rather easily, evaluate the performance of your incumbents compared with these behaviors. But how do you evaluate the behaviors of candidates? Use the following steps:

◆ Direct experience with the candidate by someone on your board

◆ Direct experience with the candidate by someone you know and trust in the community

◆ Insights you gain during the screening interview

Diversity (pluralism) is ethically and morally right. And research proves that diversity is good business practice.

The point is, people experience life differently. And different life experiences produce different insights and opinions that are essential and useful. What is diversity? Race/ethnicity, gender and generation, socioeconomic status, faith, sexual orientation, and more.

The most effective organizations are comfortable talking about diversity. The most effective organizations welcome pluralism and proactively seek it out.

Here's a real-life example of using diversity screens: The board identified the skills gap it needed to fill. The board reviewed its diversity. And then the board clearly summarized... We need individuals with knowledge, skills, expertise in fund development, accounting, and governance. But we will not consider any white women over fifty years of age at this time.

Behaviors (from 1 to 5, with 5 being the most positive)

Board Member Name	Focuses on Good of Agency Independent of Personal Agenda, Self-Interest, or Influence of Others	Complies with Agency's Policies, Procedures for Conducting Business—and Helps Others Do the Same	Keeps Agency Deliberations Confidential	Supports Decisions Once Made	Participates in Professional Development Opportunities	Participates in Conversation without Dominating	Behaves in Ways That Respect, Honor, and Support Group Effectiveness	Accountable for Own Performance and Fulfills Commitments	Behaves respectfully and Candidly with Others	What Else Would You Add?
1.										
2.										
3.										
4.										
5.										
6.										
7.										
8.										
Etc.										

In Summary

1. Identify the skill gaps and determine the priorities.

2. Describe diversity within the board. Identify the "gaps" in diversity. Use diversity screens to recruit candidates. You look for individuals with the skills and behaviors you need—and you look for these individuals within the diverse communities that you seek.

3. Describe the networks/connections within the board. This includes but is not limited to business, social, civic, government, faith/secular, agency customers, etc. Identify the "gaps" in networks. Use a network screen to identify candidates too.

Appendix C

Performance Appraisal Tool for the Individual Board Member

Please return by _____ to the governance committee. Thank you.

Name _____ Date _____

Section One. To Be Completed by the Agency Office

Board term: Start date _____ Class of _____

Status of term limit:

❑ First term; eligible for second three-year term

❑ Second term; ineligible for an additional term

Last review date: _____

Performance Responsibility	Year One of Term	Year Two of Term	Year Three of Term
1. Regularly attend board meetings (attendance compared with total held as of date of evaluation).			
2. Regularly attend committee/task force meetings (attendance compared with total held as of date of evaluation).			

Performance Responsibility	Year One of Term	Year Two of Term	Year Three of Term
3. Give a personal financial contribution (it is hoped that each individual will give at a personally meaningful level) (yes/no/not applicable yet).			
4. Attended board orientation (yes/no).			
5. Participate in performance appraisal of executive director (yes/no/not applicable yet).			
6. Participate in own performance appraisal as individual board member (yes/no/not applicable yet).			
7. Participate in governance assessment of the board of directors (yes/no/not applicable yet).			

Committee/task force service for the current year:

1. _____

2. _____

3. _____

Special service (e.g., officer, chair of committee/task force, special task, etc.—please list all applicable):

1. _____

2. _____

3. _____

Section Two. Your Self-Evaluation

The responsibilities below are all articulated in the organization's board member performance expectations.

Please think about your own service as a board member. Please respond candidly as you consider your participation. Thank you.

Responsibility	Yes	Needs Improvement
1. I prepare well for all board and committee meetings by reading the appropriate materials and bringing them to the meeting.		
2. I arrive on time and remain until the end of the board and committee meetings.		
3. I actively participate in board meetings (not just attend but participate in conversation).		
4. I use my personal expertise/experience in a manner that sheds light on particular issues brought before the board.		
5. I foster a healthy balance of authority between the board and chief executive officer.		
6. I understand that the CEO is accountable to the full board, not any individual board member(s,) and I behave accordingly.		
7. I share any concerns I have about the organization's program, its operations, and staff performance within the board meeting, not outside.		
8. I bring issues to the boardroom and discourage behind-the-scenes conversations that disrupt group process.		
9. I demonstrate respect and care for others in meetings and in all other situations.		
10. I work well with other board and committee members to ensure group effectiveness.		
11. I focus on governance and avoid management.		
12. I participate candidly in conversation at board and committee meetings without dominating.		
13. I listen in order to understand, not to debate.		
14. I ask strategic questions during board and committee meetings.		
15. I am brief rather than repetitive, and I move on when the board or committee is ready to move on.		

Responsibility	Yes	Needs Improvement
16. I help bring conversation to a close.		
17. I embrace the concept of unity of voice for the board, and I support decisions once made.		
18. I am sufficiently familiar with the organization's policies, programs, and finances to help make informed decisions.		
19. I help identify, cultivate, and recruit others to participate in the organization in various ways, including committee and board membership and donors of time and money.		
20. I am satisfied that there are no substantive conflicts of interest in my service as a board member.		
21. I maintain the confidentiality of the organization's business.		
22. I feel comfortable with my fellow board members, thus allowing me to work effectively as part of the collective.		
23. In the space below, please describe how you help the organization raise charitable contributions. Consider such activities as service on fund development committees or task forces; identifying the predisposed and qualifying them as prospects; nurturing relationships; soliciting gifts; etc.		
24. Please evaluate the organization's support to you as an individual board member.		
a. I receive the support, resources, and tools necessary to perform effectively as a board member.		
b. I am offered opportunities to learn and grow as a board member.		
c. I feel adequately informed about governance issues (including finance, program, etc.) in order to fulfill my legal and moral responsibility as part of the board of directors.		

25. In summary:

    a. I believe that I fulfill my obligation as a board member based on the performance responsibilities that were presented to me when I was recruited.

        ❑ Very well

        ❑ Satisfactorily

        ❑ Needs improvement

    b. Please rate your overall performance in the areas applicable to you.

	Very Good	Satisfactory	Needs Improvement
Board member			
Committee chair			
Committee member			
Officer			

    c. What have been your most meaningful areas of service as a board member?

26. Is your service as a board member rewarding?

    To what extent has your service as a board member been stimulating and rewarding to you?

    ❑ To a great extent

    ❑ To some extent

    ❑ To a little extent

    Please comment on your response:

27. How do you plan to become a more effective board member?

    a. My strengths as a board member are:

    b. Areas that would benefit from enhancement in my performance as a board or committee member are:

    c. What can the organization do to help you become a more effective board member?

    d. I work to develop my own skills so that I might take a leadership role.

      ❑ Yes

      ❑ I am not interested in a leadership role.

28. How can we all work together to strengthen the board and individual board member performance?

    a. What do you view as the board's greatest strengths?

    b. Conversely, what areas do you think the board needs to improve?

29. Do you have any comments on this evaluation process?

Appendix D

Comparing Performance Expectations with Actual Performance: Another Version of Board Member Assessment

Keep in mind that self-assessment is not good enough. Research shows that poor performers tend to evaluate themselves highly. Combine self-assessment with assessment by the governance committee.

Performance Expectation (as articulated in the board-adopted policy and shared with and agreed to by the candidates)	Actual Performance Results (scale of 1 to 10)		
	1–2: Problem	3–6: Needs Improvement	7–10: Okay to Good
1. Believe in and be an active advocate and ambassador for the values, mission, and vision of the organization.			
2. Act in a way that contributes to the effective operation of the board—and work with fellow board members and staff to ensure that the board functions well. This includes but is not necessarily limited to the following:			
a. Focus on the good of the organization, independent of personal agenda, self-interest, or influence of others.			
b. Support the organization's policies and procedures for conducting business.			

Performance Expectation (as articulated in the board-adopted policy and shared with and agreed to by the candidates)	Actual Performance Results (scale of 1 to 10)		
	1–2: Problem	3–6: Needs Improvement	7–10: Okay to Good
c. Maintain confidentiality of committee, board, and organization work unless authorized otherwise.			
d. Support board decisions once they are made.			
3. Participate in professional development opportunities to strengthen corporate governance and advance the organization's effectiveness through learning.			
4. Participate in appraisal of own performance and the performance of the board and its committees.			
5. Regularly attend board and committee meetings. Prepare for these meetings by reviewing materials and bringing the materials to meetings. Use conversation as a core business practice, asking strategic questions and participating in dialogue.			
6. Participate in opportunities to engage in/understand the organization's mission.			
7. Help support the charitable contributions operation of the organization. Specifically:			
a. Reach into diverse communities and help identify and cultivate relationships to support the organization as donors, volunteers, and advocates.			

Performance Expectation (as articulated in the board-adopted policy and shared with and agreed to by the candidates)	Actual Performance Results (scale of 1 to 10)		
	1–2: Problem	3–6: Needs Improvement	7–10: Okay to Good
b. Give an annual financial contribution to the best of your personal ability. If the organization launches a special campaign, give to that too. (Some organizations make this type of statement: "Consider this organization one of your top two or three charitable commitments."			
c. Participate in fund development by taking on various tasks tailored to your comfort and skills.			
8. As appropriate, use personal and professional contacts and expertise to benefit the organization without compromising ethics or trespassing on relationships. (Each candidate is invited to join the board in order to provide specific expertise to the governance process. The individual is informed of this need—and agrees—prior to nomination or appointment.)			
9. Be available to serve as a committee/task force chair or member. Be a prepared and active participant.			
10. Inform the board of directors of any potential conflicts of interest, whether real or perceived, and abide by the decision of the board related to the situation.			

Performance Expectation (as articulated in the board-adopted policy and shared with and agreed to by the candidates)	Actual Performance Results (scale of 1 to 10)		
	1–2: Problem	3–6: Needs Improvement	7–10: Okay to Good
11. Respect the authority of the chief executive officer and staff, and adhere to the limitations of the board, its committees, and individual board members.			
12. Agree to step down from board position if unable to fulfill these expectations.			

Index

M

missed meetings, bylaws, 68–69

N

nominating committee, 11

O

officers, 31, 43, 64
organizational culture, 7–10,
14–15, 47, 60–61, 65
organizational values, 41, 43, 53

P

performance appraisal tools,
12–13, 64
**performance expectations of
board members,** 13, 61, 65

S

self-assessment, board, 12, 38
self-firing, 73

If you enjoyed this book, you'll want to pick up the other books in the CharityChannel Press **In the Trenches™** series.

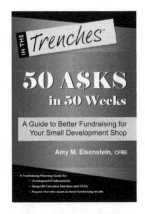

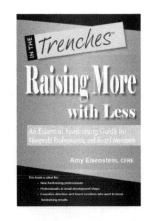

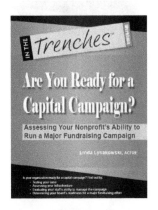

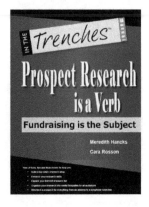

CharityChannel.com/bookstore

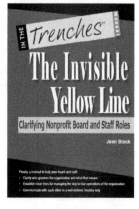

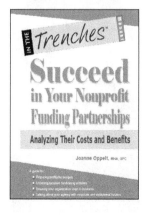

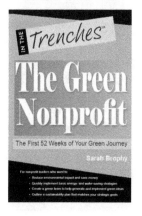

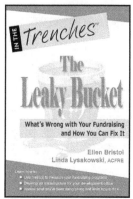

CharityChannel.com/bookstore

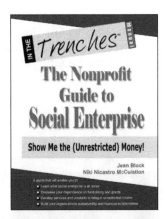

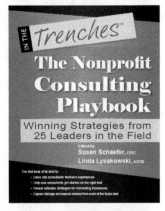

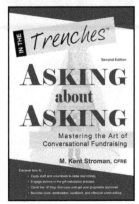

CharityChannel.com/bookstore

And now introducing **For the GENIUS® Press,** an imprint that produces books on just about any topic that people want to learn. You don't have to be a genius to read a **GENIUS** book, but you'll sure be smarter once you do!

ForTheGENIUS.com/bookstore

ForTheGENIUS.com/bookstore

PRESS

Fundraising

for the GENIUS™

The only book you'll ever need
to raise more money for your
nonprofit organization.

FOR THE GENIUS IN ALL OF US™

Linda Lysakowski, ACFRE

ForTheGENIUS.com/bookstore

P R E S S

CPSIA information can be obtained
at www.ICGtesting.com
Printed in the USA
FFHW020429200519
52537345-57980FF